ONE SIGNAL
PUBLISHERS

ATRIA

The Fight of Our Lives

MY TIME WITH ZELENSKYY, UKRAINE'S BATTLE FOR DEMOCRACY, AND WHAT IT MEANS FOR THE WORLD

IULIIA MENDEL

TRANSLATED BY MADELINE G. LEVINE

ONE SIGNAL
PUBLISHERS

ATRIA

NEW YORK • LONDON • TORONTO • SYDNEY • NEW DELHI

ONE SIGNAL
PUBLISHERS

ATRIA

An Imprint of Simon & Schuster, Inc.
1230 Avenue of the Americas
New York, NY 10020

Based on Iuliia Mendel's book, *"Кожен із нас Президент,"*
Книжковий клуб "Клуб Сімейного Дозвілля," 2021.
A subsequent Russian version was translated into English by Madeline G. Levine.

First One Signal Publishers/Atria Books hardcover edition September 2022

ONE SIGNAL PUBLISHERS / ATRIA BOOKS and colophon are
trademarks of Simon & Schuster, Inc.

For information about special discounts for bulk purchases,
please contact Simon & Schuster Special Sales at 1-866-506-1949
or business@simonandschuster.com.

The Simon & Schuster Speakers Bureau can bring authors to your live event.
For more information or to book an event, contact the Simon & Schuster
Speakers Bureau at 1-866-248-3049 or visit our website at www.simonspeakers.com.

Interior design by Dana Sloan

Manufactured in the United States of America

1 3 5 7 9 10 8 6 4 2

Library of Congress Control Number: 2022938202

ISBN 978-1-6680-1271-0
ISBN 978-1-6680-1273-4 (ebook)

At the trial of God, we will ask: why did you allow all this?
And the answer will be an echo: why did you allow all this?

—ILYA KAMINSKY, *DEAF REPUBLIC*

CONTENTS

BRIEF TIMELINE OF MODERN, INDEPENDENT UKRAINE

1990: The Revolution on Granite, considered the first major political protest in Ukraine against its continuation as part of the Union of Soviet Socialist Republics (USSR), the unitary communist state dominated by Russia and including Ukraine, that resulted from the 1917 Bolshevik Revolution.

August 24, 1991: The collapse of the USSR. Ukrainian declaration of independence, confirmed by popular referendum on December 1.

June–July 1994: First presidential election of the new Ukrainian government. Former prime minister Leonid Kuchma defeats incumbent president Leonid Kravchuk. First peaceful transfer of political power in independent Ukraine.

December 5, 1994: Budapest Memorandum on Security Assurances. The memorandum prohibited the Russian Federation, the United Kingdom, and the United States from threatening or using military force or economic coercion against Ukraine, Belarus, and Kazakhstan, "except in self-defense or otherwise in accordance with the Charter of the United Nations."

1996: The Constitution of Ukraine is enacted and the Ukrainian currency hryvnia (UAH) is adopted.

2004–2005: The Orange Revolution. Ukrainians hold massive protests against corruption and electoral fraud during the presidential election.

2013–2014: The Revolution of Dignity. Ukrainians again protest corruption and their leader Viktor Yanukovych's refusal to sign a free trade agreement with the European Union, demanding that Ukraine join the European Union and claim its place as part of Europe. They reject Russian pressure to form closer ties with the Russian Federation. Yanukovych is deposed and goes to live in Russia.

February–March 2014: The annexation of the Ukrainian peninsula of Crimea by Russia.

April 2014: The start of the Russian military invasion of Donbas (including the two areas of Donetsk and Luhansk), which results in the Russian occupation of part of that region.

June 2014: The Normandy Format group is established to negotiate a settlement to end the conflict. It includes leaders from Ukraine, France, Germany, and Russia, who first meet during the events marking the seventieth anniversary of the Allied landings in Normandy on D-Day. Five meetings occur between 2014 and 2016.

June 8, 2014: The Trilateral Contact Group on Ukraine, a group of representatives from Ukraine, Russia, and the Organization for Security and Co-operation in Europe, is established as a means to facilitate a diplomatic resolution to the war in Donbas, a region of Ukraine.

September 2014: The Minsk Protocol significantly reduces fighting in the conflict zone of Donbas. The negotiations to achieve this agreement are held in Minsk, the capital of Belarus.

February 2015: The Package of Measures for the Implementation of the Minsk Agreements, commonly called Minsk II, is signed, but never enforced by Russia.

2016–2019: Normandy Format negotiations stall for three years.

December 2019: The last full Normandy meeting, which includes the presidents of Ukraine, France, and Russia, and the German chancellor. There is one further meeting in Paris in April 2021, which the Russian president does not attend.

April 2021: Russia starts mobilizing troops along the borders of

Ukraine, amassing an estimated 150,000 to 200,000 troops near the east, south, and north of Ukraine, including in the territory of Belarus that borders Ukraine in the north.

February 21, 2022: Russia recognizes the so-called Donetsk People's Republic and the Luhansk People's Republic, two self-proclaimed statelets in Donbas controlled by pro-Russian separatists.

February 24, 2022: Russia invades Ukraine. Multipronged offensives are launched from Russia, Belarus, and the two occupied territories of Ukraine (Crimea and Donbas). The four major fronts are the Kyiv offensive, the northeastern Ukraine offensive, the eastern Ukraine offensive, and the southern Ukraine offensive. Russian missiles hit multiple Ukrainian cities and Russian airplanes drop bombs, targeting military infrastructure and airports, and also civilian targets, while artillery and armored vehicles shell civilian infrastructure such as hospitals, schools, restaurants, malls, and homes, killing thousands of Ukrainians. The invasion triggers Europe's largest refugee crisis since World War II, with around six million Ukrainians leaving the country and at least seven million others displaced inside Ukraine.

A NOTE FROM THE AUTHOR

Ukraine is an ancient land, inhabited since prehistoric times. We Ukrainians can trace our European roots back more than a thousand years to a settlement where Kyiv now stands. From that first settlement, a great medieval state was born, later known as Kyivan Rus'.

Over the centuries, the vast territory of Ukraine, with its rich agricultural land, its steppes, seacoasts, and forests, weathered incursions from both land and sea, and from nearly every direction. It endured and outlasted temporary rule by invading powers, many attempting to suppress and dominate our people. Though these empires are long gone, traces of them remain in our unique Ukrainian culture, in our proud identity as a multiethnic, multireligious European nation.

We are a proud people with a stubborn will to endure as a free, independent country. We are united in our desire to determine our own future as a democratic nation, the future that began in 1991 when Ukraine declared its independence from the disintegrating, Russian-dominated Union of Soviet Socialist Republics (the USSR) and set out boldly on its new path. That is where my own story—and the story of independent Ukraine—began.

Now we are facing a new invasion from a barbaric foe. Our very existence is at stake, but our will to be free will not die.

"I Need Ammunition, Not a Ride"

KYIV, FEBRUARY 24, 2022

I woke up to the sounds of explosions and air-raid sirens. My boyfriend, Pavlo, an adviser to the Ministry of Energy, and I knew they were coming. The night before, our friend Anton Gerashchenko, the adviser to the interior minister, had told us that the Russians would start their invasion by morning. Anton said we had less than twenty-four hours. He was right.

My stomach went into spasms and my head filled with fog. After the first shock, adrenaline kicked in. I went online immediately to find out what was happening and saw that Vladimir Putin's "special operation to denazify Ukraine" had begun at 4:00 a.m., reminiscent of the German invasion of Ukraine during World War II on June 22, 1941, which started at the same time. My mom called at 5:00 a.m. She was in complete disbelief. She told me that there were explosions around my hometown, Kherson, a city about four hundred miles south of Kyiv near the

Black and Azov Seas where I grew up and my parents still live. Other relatives I talked to confirmed what she said. By 6:00 a.m., when Putin went on TV to officially confirm the invasion, tanks were already moving into Ukraine in the east. Russian warplanes had begun to bomb depots and infrastructure and even civilian homes in sixteen regions of the country.

I turned on the TV. Russia-24, Ukraine 24, CNN, and other online media such as Ukayinska Pravda had all erupted with stories about what was happening in our country in the east, south, north, center, and even west. Enormous amounts of propaganda dispersed through Russian media justified the Russians' brutal and cynical invasion. They were bombing everywhere. Seeing all the disinformation on Russian media, I started tweeting in the hope of getting out the truth about what was happening. Journalists began calling me at around noon, and I did interview after interview with media from many countries. Many knew how to reach me from my time as the press secretary to the president of Ukraine, a position I had left less than a year before.

My brain still refused to accept this new reality, even as it registered the sounds of the explosions and the air-raid sirens. Pavlo and I had packed emergency bags in anticipation of this moment, but we hadn't yet bothered to check out where the bomb shelters were in our neighborhood. Local authorities had given us a map to local shelters weeks before, but we hadn't been able to get our minds around having to use it.

Our small studio apartment was located in the leafy southern part of the city in a student area with big apartment blocks. Outside, through our windows, we could see the park and the highway, where a traffic jam started to form almost immediately. People raced to flee the city. We decided to stay longer, using the time to fill our car with gas and make sure we packed our clothes and medicines. We could not bear to eat anything but managed to drink some water. We were so tense.

The next morning, after a troubled sleep, the explosions woke me again. I shot up and yelled, "Get up! Run! Run!" They were deafening now. It felt like rockets were about to come right through our window. The fighting sounded much closer than yesterday, and outside our window, we saw once more the long line of cars leaving the city. That is when my boyfriend and I decided we must leave Kyiv and go to the western Ukrainian city of Lviv.

We set off with our two cats, Marusia and Hooligan, and joined the long line of cars headed out of the city. It was very slow going, with traffic stopped altogether about sixty miles from Lviv because, we were told, priority had been given to the movement of military equipment. Most of the gas stations we passed were out of fuel, and there were so many checkpoints along the way. At some point we left the main route and, traveling by rural back roads, finally reached our destination—normally a five-to-seven-hour trip—forty hours later. We had arranged to stay in Lviv at an apartment with some friends. The next day, we walked around the city to see how things had held up. The streets were mostly empty, except for people lined up in front of military recruitment offices and buying supplies for the war ahead.

That night, Pavlo had some surprises. First, he told me he was going to try to enlist. I started to cry. I admired his courage and loved him even more. And I realized that he had waited to bring me to safety in Lviv before he told me what he felt he must do. Then he pulled a ring out of his pocket and asked me to marry him. I felt so many emotions at once. My biggest thought, though, was that this war must come to an end. We had other plans now.

But first we had to try to help our country any way we could. I began to give several interviews a day to media outlets around the world, trying to paint an accurate picture of what was happening to us in Ukraine. I needed, above all, to fight the disinformation that was being fed by our invaders, the Russian Federation and its sympathizers. Pavlo, unable at first to join the military, got to work helping with the distribution of humanitarian aid.

For many of our fellow Ukrainians this was the second time escaping to safety. In 2014, Russia had brazenly annexed the entire Ukrainian peninsula of Crimea overnight and occupied part of the east of Ukraine, in the region of Donbas. Ukrainian soldiers and volunteers rallied to defend Donbas back then, and during that conflict about fourteen thousand had died. That war rendered millions of Ukrainians homeless and turned them into internally displaced persons nearly overnight. This time, however, Pavlo and I joined the millions more pushed from their homes, on the move, fleeing toward Western Europe.

Suddenly, our nation's very existence was imperiled. Russians were bombarding our nation's capital. Having amassed more than 150,000 troops on Ukraine's borders in the previous ten months, the Russian military surrounded my country from the south, east, and north and had also mobilized troops in neighboring Belarus.

It all simply would not register. Our minds raced, trying to make sense of what was happening around us. We knew Russia's invasion had been coming and yet we didn't. We knew of the troop buildup on the border, and the United States had shared abundant intelligence about an imminent invasion, yet for most Ukrainians, this was all but unthinkable. Less than a month earlier, on January 28, 2022, President Zelenskyy had held a news conference, urging people not to panic and to keep going to work, as our country struggled to emerge from the downturn caused by COVID-19. Ukrainian intelligence officials projected many scenarios—but a full-scale ground invasion, which was now unfolding, was never seriously considered. The army had conducted drills and was ready to fight. Local authorities had prepared bomb shelters. But little had been communicated to our citizens about what to do in the event the Russians actually invaded.

In the midst of these preparations, the U.S. military had received intelligence that the Russians planned to surround Kyiv, assassinate Zelenskyy, and install a puppet regime. It offered to help him flee Ukraine. But when I heard this, I knew that he would never agree to go. I had seen his courage when I had accompanied him on trips to visit soldiers on the front lines in Donbas, during the ongoing conflict there. He would insist on going to the most forward, dangerous positions, to chat with soldiers and shake their hands as the shells landed nearby. Once, he took the president of Switzerland to a bridge where armed Russian-backed separatists stood just on the other side. So I was not surprised when I heard his now famous retort to the United States' offer after the invasion: "The fight is here. I need ammunition, not a ride." The comment ricocheted around the globe, galvanized Ukrainians, and earned the world's admiration.

On February 25, the day after the invasion started and with the Russians having already breached the city limits of Kyiv, Zelenskyy posted a reassuring video of himself with all the members of the Ukrainian leadership, standing outside on a street in downtown Kyiv as if it were the safest place in the world:

Good evening, everyone. The leader of the presidential party is here. The head of the presidential office is here. Prime Minister [Denys] Shmyhal is here. [Mykhailo] Podoliak [adviser to the head of the presidential office] is here. The president is here. We are all here. Our service members are here. Citizens are here. We are all here protecting our independence and our country, and it will stay like that. Glory to the heroes, glory to Ukraine.

President Zelenskyy's popularity, which had been declining, soared once the war started. Perhaps he had not always been a perfect leader. There had been difficulty in mustering the necessary support around his initiatives, managing his staff, and navigating the shoals of partisan politics. But in the chaos of war he knew exactly what to do. He became our national protector. He lifted our spirits and calmed our nerves. He rallied the army, the Ukrainian people, and everyone who was appalled by the Russians' inhumane and terrifying aggression.

During those dangerous days and in the lengthening weeks of war, Zelenskyy spoke to almost every world leader and gave addresses to parliaments on nearly every continent on the planet, displaying a moral clarity that has seldom been seen since World War II. "We ask for a response. For the response from the world. For the response to terror," he told the U.S. Congress. He echoed Winston Churchill to the British Parliament: "We shall not give up and shall not lose." His words and actions inspired admiration and support not just from his countrymen but from people everywhere. Those who had discounted Zelenskyy in the past were amazed that this post-Soviet former comedian, the leader of the poorest country in Europe, could suddenly become the face of democracy and a beacon of freedom in the world.

Zelenskyy's wife, Olena, rallied the country as well. She had remained in Ukraine, too, along with their two children, ages seventeen and nine, though at a different, undisclosed location apart from his. She communicated with her husband only by telephone during the first months of the war. Since the invasion began, she had been using her influence to help her fellow citizens, posting supportive messages online and appealing for aid to Ukraine's women and children. She had added her voice to Zelenskyy's appeals to close the skies and brought special attention to the large numbers of Ukraine's youngest victims who had been wounded or killed by the Russians (around four hundred children in the first month of the war). She posted videos of hospitals filled with the wounded, images of women in their military uniforms, and black-and-white pictures with the names of the children who had died, in an effort to put a human face on what had been lost.

In the first weeks after the Russian tanks crossed our border, we witnessed a complete reversal of the world order that had been in place since World War II. Historically neutral Switzerland forgot its neutrality. Germany, which had previously defended the nearly completed Nord Stream 2, a pipeline bringing natural gas from Russia to Germany, halted its certification and began arms production. The Russian Central Bank came under sanctions, and the Russian banks were cut off from the SWIFT bank transfer system, restricting their access to banks across the world. All the shiny global brands were fleeing from Russia to save their reputations, and foreigners poured their Russian vodka down the drain. Russia had quickly alienated itself from Europe, the United States, and many other parts of the world community.

Nevertheless, Putin remained undeterred. He was determined to strike a blow at the West, to show his limitless power, and to avenge the supposed humiliation inflicted on the Russian people since the fall of the Soviet Union in 1991. The Russian Federation continued its invasion by cruelly and relentlessly bombing Ukrainian cities, killing and maiming innocent civilians, and creating Europe's worst humanitarian crisis in recent years. In the first two weeks of the war alone, Russia fired 710 missiles into Ukraine, bombing schools, apartment buildings, and hospitals. The Russian military shelled a theater being used as a civilian shelter filled with more than a thousand women and children.

This unthinkable catastrophe is devastating our country today and will probably continue for some months to come, but all of us in Ukraine are undeterred. We are determined to have a different future. We were given that future three decades ago, on August 24, 1991, when I was almost five years old, the day Ukraine officially declared its independence from the Soviet Union. It was a monumental achievement after seventy years of Communist rule. For me, it meant that, suddenly, overnight, I no longer had to grow up with limited choices. Instead, I could believe that anything was possible, if I was willing to work hard.

The history of independent Ukraine is therefore also my story. I am a child of the new Ukraine, the only person in my family whose native language is Ukrainian. I was lucky to be born at the right time. I had the chance to get a good education: born a provincial girl, I earned a doctorate in Ukrainian literature, worked as a journalist, and then became President Zelenskyy's press secretary before returning to journalism. I proudly earned my place in a prosperous, thriving, free, and transparent country.

This is also the story of a generation—my generation—and those who think like us. We are determined to restore our lost Ukrainian heritage while we also construct a vibrant contemporary identity. We have plenty of ideas about where we are headed, what we value from the past, and who we will be in decades to come.

The story of Ukrainian society can teach others a great deal. Our identity is complicated, multifaceted, multiethnic, multireligious, and tolerant, and it melds both ancient wisdom and romantic ideals. We have endured so much: slavery under the tsars, discrimination, and poverty. We have suffered extreme hardship, surviving both the Holodomor, a Soviet state-sponsored famine in the 1930s that killed millions, and the Holocaust and World War II, which together killed several million more. For these past three decades, it has not been easy to live in constant crisis, to lose territories, to be subject to security guarantees, and at the same time to speak about a country of possibilities and opportunities, of our rich history, our national heroes, and the culture of our ancestors. But that's the way it is. We know who we are, and we will not let others define us.

We are not victims.

We are a country where people manage to live together with their grudges and completely different pasts, sometimes with polar-opposite worldviews, but with a determination to create a rich mosaic of cultures.

Yet these traumas have taken their toll. Psychologists Carol Dweck and Lauren Howe at Stanford University have written about the "trauma of the rejected": how, after rejection, a person may question his or her own right to exist. Remember how in school, arriving late, some students would knock politely at the door, timidly look around, and apologize, attempting to avoid attention? And others would burst in like a whirlwind, completely confident that they had a place? Ukrainians resemble those timid pupils. Our lack of confidence is in response to the numerous attempts to erase Ukraine as a nation. The time has come for us to have faith in ourselves.

Volodymyr Zelenskyy showed us that we can be different: confident, powerful, with a seat at the table. He ran for president and won by showing us that we belong in this twenty-first century. We exist. Here and now. Independent and strong. And we will have a role in the future of our planet.

Working with President Zelenskyy during the first two years of his administration, I had a ringside seat at some of the most dramatic moments in the history of modern Ukraine. I watched as a popular young TV comedian and his colleagues were swept into power after a landslide election victory, promising to make real change in Ukraine. While these untested leaders had a rocky start, eventually they began to challenge the power of the oligarchs who controlled the Ukrainian economy and curb some of the rampant corruption at every level of society. They pushed back against Russian interference in Ukrainian politics and tried to end the war of Russian aggression in eastern Ukraine. But then a much bigger war came, the one we had long feared—an existential threat, not just for Ukraine but for the project of democracy throughout the world.

This book is a record of what I observed during these turbulent, horrific, and ultimately hopeful years in our history, taking into account all that I and other Ukrainians like me have experienced until now and what we see as our legacy as we battle against the Russian invaders each day. It's also a heroic tale about confronting a brutal dictator and his savage army, a David-and-Goliath struggle for freedom and democracy. While I can't be sure yet, I hope it will have a happy ending.

The Fight of Our Lives

CHAPTER 1

Zelenskyy's Landslide Victory

It was 7:00 a.m. on a sleepy morning in December 2020. The Wi-Fi in my apartment in Kyiv wasn't working, so I used my cellphone's 3G connection. Scrolling through the YouTube Music playlist on my phone, full of vintage post-Soviet hits, I picked Yevgeniy Belousov's "Girly Girl," a hugely popular song from the early 1990s. My master plan for sticking to my diet all day was boiling two eggs for breakfast and having buckwheat for lunch.

The playlist smoothly switched over to ten- and twenty-year-old hits, interspersed with irritating commercials for cheap local real estate. The water I'd put on for my morning tea reached a boil, steam curling up toward the ceiling, but in an instant all this turned into something unreal, unimportant. It was as if everything had entered a different dimension and no longer concerned me at all.

Suddenly, at the forty-seventh second of the Russian pop king Philipp Kirkorov's song about how April was awakening in his soul, Volodymyr Zelenskyy shot into view on my phone screen, running at full speed. Long before Zelenskyy had thought about going into politics, he was an actor, and here he was, in a 2009 music video, shown in a clip taken from one of his most popular films: young, laid-back, sincere, diligent, and in love. He was wearing a tie and a light gray suit—things I knew him to almost never wear in real life. The unexpected "visit" from my boss automatically jumped me from a relaxed state into full work mode. Those few seconds shook me out of my sleepiness and brought the day's political realities into sharp focus.

I finished my boiled eggs with sliced avocado, put the buckwheat and smoked Norwegian fish into a container for lunch, and went through my morning routines. But I did all this mechanically, as if my body were moving without my conscious participation: a shower in a stall without a waterproof door, a face cream from a new cosmetologist, black slacks and a black sweater, and a mountain of messages in WhatsApp.

There was more than enough work to do, and I knew that Zelenskyy was paying close attention to the communications team's work. The man in the music video in the role of a romantic hero did not bear much resemblance to the President Zelenskyy I knew, who placed exacting professional demands on himself and on his team. The same perfectionism that he had shown in his past TV production work, asking his team to shoot scenes over and over again, was now evident in how he oversaw our office's output of news, photos, and videos addressing persistent controversies that appeared in politics and vexed our young democracy.

That morning my team faced a lot of challenges at the office. There was a fight going on between the Ministry of Defense and a dogged opposition journalist, and activists were in the midst of a crusade against the deputy to the presidential office, accusing him of corruption. Also, we were approaching the anniversary of the Normandy Format meeting, where leaders of Ukraine, Germany, France, and Russia had tried but failed to resolve the conflict stemming from Russia's invasion of the Ukrainian region of Donbas in 2014.

This had not been an easy week. In fact, it had been one of the toughest of the year. By the tail end of 2020, the failures were piling up. Internal discord had led to petty conflicts among our leadership team, and irritation hung in the air. The national budget had not been passed or even approved yet by the various parties. And even if it was approved, all we could hope for was a deficit of more manageable scale. The specter of default hovered over Ukraine for the umpteenth time. We could not manage without our Western partners. They always grumbled about providing the next tranche of funding to Ukraine, but they knew that they could not abandon a country of forty million people in the heart of Europe.

Ukraine was suffering. Conflict in Donbas, delayed reforms, and deep-rooted corruption all had become part of the country's mental outlook over the past thirty years, since the breakup of the Soviet Union and the founding of our independent state. Our society was fragmenting into two groups: those who were inclined toward a Western mindset, and those who were more pro-Russian. This process had been going on year after year. Generations changed, but Ukraine still had not succeeded in assembling the "package" of values from which it could construct a really strong state. It was a few weeks before New Year 2020.

I cannot say that I hadn't been warned about the challenges

of this job. I'd arrived in the President's Office after a decade in journalism, spent mostly in Ukraine and then later in Brussels. I had seen up close how things were going in Ukraine and how difficult it was to make changes when there was little political will in leadership.

In 2016 in Brussels, where I had worked as an international telejournalist, I became acquainted with Matthew Kaminski, an editor at *Politico Europe*, the publication that was read by politicians in all the European Union capitals. Before that he had worked as an international correspondent, having reported for decades on several continents. He also covered events in Russia, Ukraine, and other post-Soviet countries.

"Nowhere are there such lousy politicians as in Ukraine," he once observed, so bluntly and unexpectedly that it felt like a revelation. "Of course, there is also corruption in Russia, violation of human rights, and poverty and difficult living conditions. But their politicians there still possess some core values." We were speaking in English, but he added one word in Russian that he had learned during his assignment in Moscow: *gosudarstvennost'*, "statehood." He emphasized the word. "This is what the Russian politicians believe in; it is their ideology. Ukrainian politicians have no values. They are ready to promise anything, even contradictory things, if that helps them stay in power."

If you looked closely enough, though, there were already some small cracks in that corrupt Ukrainian edifice. The Euromaidan protests—demonstrations against Viktor Yanukovych, the pro-Russian president—began in late 2013 and evolved into what became known as the Revolution of Dignity, when millions of Ukrainians rose up against corruption and rapprochement with Russia. More than one hundred people died in the crackdown that followed, sacrificing their lives for fundamental human values. In 2014, Yanukovych was forced from power and left the country. That year, and the years that followed, seemed to usher in a new political spirit. Ukraine asserted its desire to be a part of the European family of nations by signing the EU-Ukraine Association Agreement, which made the EU Ukraine's main trading partner. In 2017, Ukrainians gained permission to travel visa-free to EU countries for short stays. We undertook new reforms, and the Western press began to take note of our desires. It seemed that, given the right leadership, a great deal could change, and soon.

But progress came slowly and was barely noticeable inside the country. One-quarter of the Ukrainian population lived below the poverty line. Many villages in regions across the country still lacked indoor plumbing and gas. The average Ukrainian worker received monthly wages equivalent to $150. The press found seemingly endless stories to report about bribery and scandals involving multimillions of dollars. In just one example, in March 2017, our anti-corruption bureau detained the head of the State Tax Service of Ukraine, Roman Nasirov. He was accused of embezzlement of state tax revenues. The damage amounted to more than $74 million. He faced six years in prison, and yet he avoided jail entirely. After his arrest, his wife paid a bail of around $4 million. Nasirov was brought to trial but never went to jail. Since he was never convicted, the Central Electoral Committee allowed him to run for the presidency in the 2019 election. This brazen move, however, did not win him much support; he finished last among the thirty-nine recognized candidates. Nasirov, like many of Ukraine's old political elites, proclaimed his pro-European orientation, but not for even a minute did he want to become European himself, or accountable to anyone.

In 2019 those who surrounded Ukraine's then incumbent president Petro Poroshenko were mired in corruption scandals and hypocrisy. They embraced outmoded, conservative ideas and resisted change. Just as before, the strong became stronger, and the supercilious elites reveled in their privileged status. The rest of us watched wearily and with increasing irritation. Becoming more like Europe remained beyond reach for us without European-style politicians. President Poroshenko's team were still the same Soviet swindlers we had endured before, feeding at the budgetary trough, enriching themselves and impoverishing the rest of us. Pretentious slogans could not conceal their Soviet-style habits. The political elite had long since become rotten, and a change of faces changed nothing.

In almost thirty years of independence, Ukrainian political parties had failed to come up with either a unified state ideology or their own ideological values. The durability of each new political party was entirely dependent on the personal appeal of its leader. The values professed, the promises made, and the actions taken were entirely determined by the profits that could be gained. No one would refuse political payoffs in order to uphold ideological values.

No political group could manage to define our Ukrainian identity, either. Poroshenko attempted to do that during his 2019 presidential campaign by returning to conservative ideals from the early twentieth century. In Poroshenko's telling, the Ukrainian army stood at the center of the nation's identity—the same army that his cronies preyed on for their own enrichment. Another focus of his was the Ukrainian language, which Poroshenko's own family did not speak. And a third was religious faith and the Ukrainian Orthodox Church's demand for autocephaly, or independence, from the Russian Orthodox Church. There were other elements of Ukrainian identity, too, that were trotted out to define us. Western journalists continued to equate Ukrainian culture with the legends of the brave Cossacks—self-governing, semimilitary communities that flourished from the fifteenth to the eighteenth century—as well as the home-baked bread that village maidens made for their weddings, and Christmas caroling from peasant house to peasant house described in Ukrainian classics. In short, for Western observers, Ukraine was identified with the peasantry and remained in their minds a post-Soviet province.

Poroshenko bought into that stereotype and chose to push the same picture of Ukraine to the world, denying the scale, multiple meanings, complexity, diversity, mixed character, and contradictory nature of contemporary Ukrainian society. The more he pushed this overly narrow definition of Ukraine, the more unnatural it seemed.

Toward the end of 2018, few were excited by the prospect of a second Poroshenko presidential term when it became clear he would run again in 2019, and another political old-timer, Yulia Tymoshenko, also declared her candidacy. The absence of real alternatives to the status quo suddenly opened up an enormous space for new possibilities. It was then that Volodymyr Zelenskyy, a TV star with no prior political experience, decided to enter the political arena.

Zelenskyy was not a politician, although he had registered his political party a year and a half earlier, using the same name as his wildly popular TV show, *Servant of the People.* In his show, Zelenskyy portrayed an ordinary schoolteacher, Vasyl Petrovych Holoborodko, who gets elected president by accident. It was art imitating life and life imitating art at the same time, and it was brilliant. The TV show aired weekly, right up to the election, and it functioned as a showcase for Zelenskyy's political ideas. And everyone watched it.

When Zelenskyy formally announced just before midnight on New Year's Eve that he was running for president in 2019, many people sighed with relief. Zelenskyy was a breath of fresh air. He provided hope that had not existed for a long time. Perhaps the only person who was unhappy with Zelenskyy's decision was his wife, Olena, a screenwriter, who did not want to live in the spotlight. She could foresee what it would mean for her and her family if Zelenskyy won the election. As she observed in 2019 in *Vogue Ukraine*, "I prefer staying backstage. My husband is always on the forefront, while I feel more comfortable in the shade." And though she was able to keep much of her family life private, after Zelenskyy's election, she grew to appreciate how she could use her influence for good. During my years as press secretary, I saw how attentive Zelenskyy was to her, often checking in with her on official trips and making sure to keep her by his side. In fact, he wanted her to be there with him at those crucial moments, his partner in all things.

During the presidential campaign, possibly for the first time in his life, Zelenskyy felt what it meant to be *unloved*. He was accustomed to being idolized like a pop star, first as an ardent and active university student, then as a cheerful and quick-witted comedian on a post-Soviet show (cleverly named *KVN*, the Russian abbreviation for *Club of the Funny and Resourceful*) and, more recently, in every new comedy program and film.

For four fast-moving months, Zelenskyy experienced what it felt like to have political opponents sling mud at him, constantly and sometimes successfully looking for compromising information. He also learned what it meant to debate in public without a teleprompter, a skill he soon mastered, thanks to his many years of stage experience.

This neophyte politician quickly rose to the challenge, reassuring crowds of voters, taking stock of his competition, and examining the new world around him. His empathy and command onstage served him well when it was time for the one-on-one debates with the incumbent, Poroshenko. His political inexperience appealed to people. I observed among my family members that Zelenskyy aroused feelings of compassion—an almost parental desire to protect him.

In Ukraine, elections can be decided in one round if someone gets 50 percent plus one vote, but with thirty-nine candidates taking part, such an outcome was virtually impossible in 2019. Only Zelenskyy and Poroshenko had enough votes to make it to the second round.

Poroshenko assumed that Zelenskyy would be intimidated by a face-to-face debate with a career politician like himself. For that reason, he insisted on holding debates in 2019, a change from his strategy in the 2014 election, when he refused to grant his opponent the same opportunity.

Either choice—participating or not participating in the debates—posed a risk for Zelenskyy. When they learned of Poroshenko's challenge, Zelenskyy's team posted a video invitation to Poroshenko that proposed conditions for an as yet unplanned debate. Zelenskyy stipulated that each candidate would have to undergo a drug test beforehand in order to show he was clean, that Poroshenko had to apologize for smearing dirt on Zelenskyy, and that the debate must be held in the Olympic

Stadium—Ukraine's national sports complex—in front of a live audience and with mass media, not in a television studio as the law prescribed previous debates be held.

The video went viral. Forced to respond, Poroshenko agreed to all the conditions apart from issuing an apology for his attacks on Zelenskyy's character. His response, "Stadium? Okay, stadium," became a meme in Ukraine. This reply attempted to disguise his anxiety and demonstrated a paternalistic condescension, as if he didn't care on what platform he would "demolish" the newcomer. And it served to drive interest even higher in the two men's contest.

Until then, my aunt had been negative about Zelenskyy and the odds of him becoming president. She didn't like his bawdy humor, and she was put off by his lack of political experience. The debates changed her attitude and opinion 180 degrees. Zelenskyy's speech was fresh, and his harsh judgments about the quality of the people running the Ukrainian government seemed fair. Most people agreed with him.

"I am not your opponent," he said to Poroshenko. "I am your verdict." With every sentence, Zelenskyy the actor and businessman hammered nails into Poroshenko's political coffin. He did not boast, and he did not promise much; his instinct told him that this was the successful script he should follow.

My aunt watched the debates anxiously, increasingly convinced by the young, disarming novice standing beside the coarse and self-confident oligarch. Poroshenko had bused in throngs of people to make sure he had a crowd of supporters.

"I want Zelenskyy to win," she said after the debates. "He should become the servant of the people." My parents agreed. For the first time, without consulting each other or quarreling, my parents and I voted for the same candidate. We all wanted to live better. And if not better, then at least we wanted to live with hope, not without it.

In June 2019, a poll by the International Republican Institute showed that 48 percent of Ukrainians expected positive economic changes in the year ahead, the first year of a Zelenskyy presidency. The percentage for the same poll stood at just 14 percent ten months earlier. The people, fed up with corrupt and rotten post-Soviet politicians, wanted real change. On Election Day, Zelenskyy received 73 percent of the votes for president, and then his new party, consisting almost entirely of completely unknown political novices, scored a historic result as well, receiving 43 percent of the popular vote in the special parliamentary elections.

The record-breaking 73 percent of the votes in the second round of voting was a revolution in itself. It was a victory won without tough protests on the streets. It was simply a clear, firm, and impassioned verdict in favor of Zelenskyy and his followers. It was the first real electoral revolution in Ukraine.

Years earlier, in 2016, I had covered the political campaigns of Donald Trump and Hillary Clinton. I had since read books on cybersecurity, hacking, and disinformation. I learned about Cambridge Analytica and watched films about the new political technologies and how they worked. I knew how the political game was now played and that some basic understanding of social media was required to understand politics in the modern age, to know how personal data is collected and used, how ads are targeted, and how bot-driven campaigns can purposefully divide entire societies. These social media stratagems manipulate our greatest fears and historical traumas; they elicit painful emotions and secretly inflate them with the intent of aggressively turning one group in society against another. The underlying premise is that voters are more easily motivated to vote by anger and resentment than by unity and purpose. Those who are undecided or supporters of opposition parties must be manipulated into doubting their choices. The ills of society are deployed as instruments of the political technologists.

In Ukraine in 2019, the themes used to divide people were patriotism, language, and the question of whether to side with Western Europe or Russia in the continent's ongoing conflicts. Poroshenko's campaign team pounced on all these issues, pitting Russian-language speakers against those who spoke Ukrainian, defining some groups as more patriotic and others as less, and introducing memes calculated to upset society and distort reality. It flooded Ukrainian social media with bots, stirred dissent to bring people out onto the streets, and poured money into media and social media channels. All that made the 2019 campaign one of the dirtiest in the history of Ukraine.

Poroshenko's campaign created a polemical atmosphere. It was the same political playbook Trump had used to win the U.S. presidential election in 2016. It gave the pro-Brexit forces their victory in the U.K. But in Ukraine that strategy didn't work. In fact, it failed spectacularly. Why did the formula that worked in Western countries not work in ours? Poroshenko was, after all, an incumbent seeking reelection in a much more fragmented society.

In Ukraine, people were fed up with the kinds of controversies that almost all the country's political forces had deliberately stirred up since 2002. These strategies were devastatingly familiar to us—we didn't have a single political campaign in which attempts were not made to divide Ukrainians. So when Zelenskyy appeared with a new ideology—unification—an instinctive thirst for this ideal kicked in, a desire to live and be happy, an impulse for self-preservation and a concern for others that Ukrainians had never known before.

Zelenskyy changed Ukrainian politics forever. He "disconnected" a large portion of the Ukrainian political elite from their comfortable hold on power and attracted people from business, the arts, and television. He changed the narrative in the country, smoothing out the conflicts between warring ideologies. He presented Ukrainian identity as it really is, without pathos, but as a palette of many colors; not as a country to be pitied, but as a dynamic European democracy.

CHAPTER 2

The Poorest Country in Europe

This will be morally complicated. This will be uncomfortable for me, I will not hide that; it will depress me. But depression and discomfort will not influence my decisions. I will bury all of that inside me; there must be reforms. We have a chance.

—VOLODYMYR ZELENSKYY ON REFORMS (FROM THE AUTHOR'S TRANSCRIPTION OF AN INTERVIEW CONDUCTED BY JOSHUA YAFFA FOR HIS ARTICLE IN THE *NEW YORKER*, AUGUST 30, 2019)

Ukraine is the poorest country in Europe, and that poverty has been a significant roadblock in the growth of a strong society.

Poverty means being unable to pay for an education, or a home, or clothing, or food, or to travel to other places and experience the world. To be poor is to be trapped in your confined world without the ability to learn something new or develop as a person.

That is why it is difficult to build strong institutions in a poor country and why it is so easy to undermine those that exist. Distorting reality in a poor country is much easier than in a rich one, and even more so in the era of social media. The struggle against poverty is vital to freedom.

When I was a schoolchild, a teacher named Valentyna Datsiuk once explained to me what deprivation meant through a simple metaphor: Every person has two wings; one is physical, the other is spiritual. If a person is not utilizing the first, the physical, by working, the second, too, will be unable to function. Without the second wing, you won't fly far on just one.

Zelenskyy's family never had any experience with the worst kinds of Ukrainian poverty, such as the absence of services and goods or the food shortages that some faced in the 1990s. But Kryvyi Rih, where he spent his formative years, was by all accounts a rough working-class town. A former Stalin-era industrial hub in central Ukraine known for its metallurgical works, it had begun a sharp economic decline in the mid-1980s. A high unemployment rate followed, and the city was plagued by violence. As many as forty gangs of teenagers, known as *beguny*, roamed the streets. After the collapse of the Soviet Union in 1991, there were no organized sports, so there was little else to do but fight other adolescents.

Zelenskyy was an only child, raised in a family of Jewish intellectuals. His father, Oleksandr, was a Ukrainian computer scientist and technology professor who later became head of the Department of Cybernetics and Computing Hardware at Kryvyi Rih State University of Economics and Technology, part of Kyiv

National Economic University. His mother, Rymma, worked as an engineer.

Like many Ukrainians of those generations born in the earlier twentieth century, Zelenskyy's family had confronted terrible tragedy. Zelenskyy has talked about how his great-grandparents were massacred after the Nazis burned down their village during World War II. Their four sons had gone to fight with the Soviets. Zelenskyy's grandfather Semyon was the only one of them who survived. A colonel and war hero in the Red Army, Semyon returned to Kryvyi Rih and became head of the local police force. Known for his integrity, he was given the job of getting rid of the local crime organizations. Zelenskyy reportedly was very close to his grandparents, particularly his paternal grandfather, who had an enduring influence on him.

Zelenskyy's parents still lived in a modest apartment in Kvartal 95, the district where he was raised. Zelenskyy was very close to his parents, and having their approval had always been of paramount importance. Even as an adult, and now as president, he still felt the need to prove to them that he was doing the right thing.

Once at lunch with his team on a trip to Poland, the president asked me if my parents had ever told me they were proud of me. In our family, this type of conversation was not exactly customary. But I replied that they were proud; at least I thought they were. I realized that Zelenskyy's question revealed how important his own parents' approval was for him.

After Zelenskyy made money in business, he wanted his parents to move to Kyiv, but they refused. And they also refused to accept a car he offered to give them as a present.

To some degree, their opposition to material goods was part

of an intergenerational conflict that was widespread in post-Soviet families. They simply were not as consumerist as their children. But whatever the reason, the Zelenskyy family did not show these differences publicly.

Their son had a different approach to life. While he, too, disapproved of all the post-Soviet emphasis on consumerism, his way of life was far from ascetic. Zelenskyy was part of a new generation in Ukraine, more adventurous than their elders and less oppressed by limitations. Zelenskyy went to the local school and joined the neighborhood comedy club at age seventeen, winning all the contests. His future wife, Olena Kiyashko, an intelligent and attractive teenager, was in the same grade but in a different class, so their paths did not cross much. However, very soon after she started classes at Kryvyi Rih National University, where she studied architecture, and Zelensky began his law studies at Kryvyi Rih Economic Institute, a branch of Kyiv National Economic University, they became inseparable. Zelenskyy pursued success from an early age, demonstrating to his post-Soviet peers a new professionalism, a new sense of humor, and a new attitude toward life in general. I would say that disrupting old patterns and breaking boundaries became a habit in his life, though I'm not sure Zelenskyy himself was aware of this.

He was a meritocrat by nature and relentless about proving himself. Some people did not understand why he was always pushing against boundaries and were put off by it. But other people identified with his irreverent energy and admired it. It was never boring to be around him. He was always looking for something better. Underneath his lighthearted demeanor, there was a deep seriousness. The media, of course, generally presented Zelenskyy as a one-dimensional figure by focusing on him as a comedian. That was merely one of his talents, however. But it was certainly the most public one. Later in his life, few people remembered that he had earned a law degree with a special concentration in constitutional law.

Zelenskyy continued his comedy sketches during his time at university. He organized a team made up of friends from his hometown, including Olena, who helped write the scripts for their shows.

Even though Olena had to browbeat acquaintances to come to those first student performances, people very quickly began to seek out the talented comedians from Kryvyi Rih. Their shows became wildly popular. Professors and former students remembered them enthusiastically when I visited the university in 2019.

The group's tremendous success encouraged Zelenskyy and his friends to pursue a professional career in comedy. I'm not quite sure how his father, who was somewhat conservative about such things, took it. But Zelenskyy and his troupe started off by scraping together a little money so they could travel to other regions of the country to perform.

Zelenskyy used his talents as a scriptwriter and manager to make his way in the entertainment world. He was a perfectionist during rehearsals, making the actors repeat their lines over and over again until they were flawless.

Not surprisingly, Zelenskyy and his group managed to get on television, performing on the most popular comedy program in the former Soviet Union, the aptly named *Club of the Funny and Resourceful* (*Klub vesyólykh i nakhódchivykh*, or *KVN*). They called their team Kvartal 95, after the Kryvyi Rih neighborhood where Zelenskyy grew up and went to school.

Their humor was brash, bawdy, and contemporary, and it focused mostly on political satire.

"In honor of the three hundredth anniversary, we propose to make St. Petersburg the capital," proclaimed one actor in Zelenskyy's troupe on the *KVN* stage in St. Petersburg in 2003.

"Great! I like it! I like the sound of that: St. Petersburg is the capital of Ukraine!" Zelenskyy boldly replied, implying that Ukraine would dominate the Russian Federation. At the time, that type of humor was still allowed. It would hardly be possible today after so many years of bloody conflict between the two nations.

It is mind-boggling to imagine the effort it took to build a business empire in Ukraine in the decades from 1990 to 2010. Businesses had to deal with corruption and pressure from law enforcement. In addition, the geopolitical situation had transformed Moscow into a major entertainment center. All the successful programs that were sold to post-Soviet countries were made there. If people wanted to make it in entertainment, they did whatever it took to make their way to Moscow, like aspiring actors who gravitate to L.A. or New York City in the United States.

The comedy troupe from Kryvyi Rih was fortunate to have the chance to compete on Russian television. Kvartal 95 met with great success at the various levels of competition—except, of course, in competition with the troupes from Moscow. The powers that be in Russia could not allow a team from Moscow to lose to anyone, especially not to a group from some provincial city in Ukraine. This was the unfair and, for many, the unacknowledged side of Russia's unwillingness to allow honest competition. The deck was stacked against up-and-comers from the provinces, even though, after the fall of the Soviet Union, these provinces were no longer provinces but independent nations. Russia always had to remain the strongest state, and of course, one not-so-subtle, yet not openly acknowledged, manifestation of this was the cultural control exerted over what appeared on television.

The year 2003 was pivotal for Zelenskyy's career. He had a quarrel with Alexander Maslyakov, the head of *KVN*, rejecting the man's offer that he become a TV editor in Moscow. Russia had always been paternalistic toward other republics and assumed that any opportunities it provided to talented people from those places should be received humbly and gratefully. Zelenskyy was offered what seemed like a great opportunity, a godfather-like offer he could not refuse; it was supposed to bring him a stable income, perhaps even wealth. The moguls in Moscow felt that this was more than enough for a hick from the provinces. But part of the deal was that Zelenskyy would have to disband his troupe. The opportunity to make it in the big time was offered only to him.

Zelenskyy turned it down. In an interview in 2019, he explained that he could not imagine abandoning his team. He returned with them to Ukraine to build his production company there.

Moscow's entertainment establishment resented his decision. It even went so far as trying to ban the first full-fledged Kvartal 95 performances back in Kyiv. In 2003, that kind of interference from Moscow was still conceivable, because the ties between Russia and Ukraine were extremely tight, and the entertainment industry was very dependent on producers from Russia.

But Zelenskyy pulled it off. I don't know how the arrangements were made, how many people were involved, but Kvartal 95 became a hit at home. Moreover, later he got his own show on TV channels owned by the biggest oligarchs in Ukraine—first

Valeriy Khoroshkovskyy and then Ihor Kolomoyskyy. It was the big break he needed: by partnering with these channels, Zelenskyy managed to build that one show into a comedy empire.

Kvartal 95 produced a huge number of successful comedy shows, all of which revolved around its charismatic star, Volodymyr Zelenskyy. In addition, he worked as a producer for Inter, the biggest TV channel in Ukraine; created many movies and TV series; and became the beloved voice of Paddington Bear in the films, musicals, and cartoons. He was genuinely successful, and he was everywhere.

Zelenskyy won accolades as a dancer in pairs competitions. He would go out on the dance floor dressed up in an over-the-top outfit of bright pink silk, or a macho T-shirt, or in 1930s gangster-style pinstripes with a panama hat; do his expert moves with his partner; and win the audience's support. A notable triumph came in 2006: he and his partner were the winning couple on the Ukrainian edition of *Dancing with the Stars*. You can still see some of his performances on YouTube.

Zelenskyy's humor always included a frontal attack on corrupt politicians and on social injustice. He made fun of influencers like post-Soviet stars or oligarchs and took aim at almost all Ukrainian politicians and even their pets. One of the targets of Zelenskyy's humorous barbs was a radical member of Ukraine's parliament, who was portrayed with a pitchfork while trying to avoid military service. In another sketch, Zelenskyy imitated the pet ostrich of a corrupt Ukrainian president on the run. It wasn't just the high and mighty who came under scrutiny. No one escaped his notice—or his mockery. His famous comedy roles included a policeman, a pilot, a drunkard, and a jealous husband, among others.

Zelenskyy's humor was targeted to a popular audience. In

fact, Kvartal 95 relied on burlesque and often on raunchy humor. Zelenskyy was not ashamed of below-the-belt jokes, like the famous scene of him in which he pretends to play the piano with his penis, or when he took on the persona of a gay cop messing with drivers. He tapped into everything that post-Soviet viewers found funny.

At first, Kvartal 95 invited big guest stars, often from Moscow, to perform with the company. This was a winning formula for success among Ukrainian viewers in the early 2000s, but after Russia's annexation of Crimea and the war in Donbas in 2014, Kvartal 95's tone changed, becoming very patriotic. There was no place for anything Russian anymore, except sharp satire. Zelenskyy could forgive Moscow for its condescendingly aggressive attitude toward him personally, but he was certainly not going to forgive that same attitude toward Ukraine.

The songs Zelenskyy and his troupe sang at the end of their show usually made people tear up with feelings of love for their homeland and pride in their nationality. He was beloved both for his lighthearted, often transgressive, slapstick humor and for how beautifully and confidently he and his theater company stood up for Ukraine.

After 2014, Putin, too, became the target of Kvartal 95's jokes: "It turns out that Ukraine's future depends not on Europe or America, but on whether Alina Kabaeva had a headache last night," said one famous member of the troupe, a reference to Putin's mistress, the gymnast and politician Alina Kabaeva.

And right after that line, Zelenskyy assumed the role of Kabaeva herself, dressed all in pink and angry at the Russian president for coming home late. Putin explained that he was late because he was discussing with Defense Minister Sergei Shoigu about sending troops into Ukrainian Crimea. Mocking Russia's well-known disinformation campaign after it seized the peninsula from Ukraine in 2014, claiming that the Kremlin never sent Russian troops into Crimea, Zelenskyy-Kabaeva replied, "Don't lie! I watch Russian television! There are no Russian troops in Crimea!"

The audience exploded in laughter.

And with that, Zelenskyy had made his point about Russian fake news.

Kvartal 95 made Zelenskyy a star. But it also gave him the opportunity to grow as a leader and a manager, and it helped pave his way into politics. During those years as a big-time entertainer, Zelenskyy was also regularly invited to perform for private audiences—it was a way to earn money in the entertainment industry—and in doing that, he met a lot of powerful people, including politicians and tycoons. He was able to enter Ukrainian politics as a comedian first, but to an extent that is little appreciated or remarked upon, these contacts gave him a rare insight into Ukraine's elite political class—the local and national politicians, businesspeople, media personalities and commentators, and others who occupied Ukraine's political space.

By 2016, Zelenskyy was already thinking about a political career. It had been a year since his hit TV series *Servant of the People* had premiered. There would be a second season the following year. And during the run-up to the presidential elections in 2019, there was a third season. These episodes were not mere entertainment; they were a commentary on the state of affairs in Ukraine and provided a new way of looking at the role of government in people's lives. So by the time Zelenskyy became president, the voters already knew the Kvartal 95 team's ideas about how to run a country.

There was a great difference, however, between writing the script for a TV show and overhauling the government of a nation of forty million people. It was true that Zelenskyy had succeeded brilliantly in building his comedy empire. He had been able, too, to overcome many of the obstacles that remained in dealing with the legacy of the former Soviet Union. But would he be able to transform a country? It was true he had learned how to make a decent living for himself and his family, but could he help all Ukrainians do the same? It was not going to be easy, especially for a country like his, as I've explained, with a legacy of poverty and underdevelopment.

After his election as president in 2019, Zelenskyy tried to address the problem of low living standards by bringing about macroeconomic stability to Ukraine via an ambitious program of economic reforms. Pro-oligarchic elements tried to discredit Zelenskyy's first government by attacking its economic program as "Sorosism," and deriding the efforts of President Zelenskyy's first prime minister, a pro-Western activist named Oleksiy Honcharuk. Honcharuk and other supporters of economic reform were given the mildly pejorative name "Sorosiglets," a pun combining the philanthropist billionaire George Soros's name and the word for "piglets" in both Ukrainian and Russian. The term, coined by conspiracy theorists from the pro-oligarchic media, became part of the political language.

As prime minister, Honcharuk radiated an aura of hard work and ambition, but he also became known for his mercurial mood swings and the colossal arrogance that he lavishly dispensed in parliament, eliciting well-deserved rebuffs in return. Nevertheless, his brief tenure in office was a period of great activity, when many reforms were proposed and enacted. Ukraine became known, in the West particularly, for its "turbocharged regime"; between August and the end of 2019, more than 150 bills were passed abolishing many obsolescent practices inherited from Soviet times and thereby transforming Ukraine's market economy.

That being said, Honcharuk's technocratic nature made it difficult for him to connect with people. This quality prevented him from understanding and empathizing on a human level with the kind of poverty that existed at that moment in various regions of Ukraine. His macroeconomic program may have worked in the long term, but he never figured out how to do something *immediately* to improve the lives of people who were in need.

Ultimately, though, most of the credit for these reforms should be given to the president. It was Zelenskyy who personally oversaw each reform, chose the blueprints, and made changes if he thought the bill would not pass in its initial form. He also urged parliament, most of whose members were ill-disposed toward Honcharuk, to vote for the bills.

In his dealings with parliament, Zelenskyy displayed just how unlike most leaders he would be. He listened, he built consensus, and he allowed the members to make their own decisions.

At the outset of his presidency, the new parliament had about seventy bills ready for approval. Two of the president's advisers thought that the parliamentary rules should be ignored and that the deputies should be forced to vote on the bills the first night the session opened. They would have passed, given his party's overwhelming majority. Two other advisers, however, counseled going more slowly, because there was a danger that these laws could be declared unconstitutional at a later date. Zelenskyy gathered together his majority and asked them for a show of hands. A majority opted for the slower approach.

"You voted for the second option. I'll be honest—I preferred the other," Zelenskyy told the lawmakers. "But I support your decision. I ask only that you not put this on ice. People chose us to serve them. People need changes."

Debate dragged on for months, but the bills eventually passed.

With so many reform bills pushed through the parliament in 2019, the future looked hopeful. Unfortunately, however, the next year proved to be far more challenging on numerous fronts. And the infighting and inexperience of many on the presidential team began to take their toll.

The presidential office was a stressful environment. There was always a high level of activity. Zelenskyy drank endless cups of coffee and didn't seem to need much sleep. Rising very early, he was in the habit of making work calls between 6:00 and 7:00 a.m., not only to his staff but also to parliament members, ministers, and other officials and politicians. I would often get texts from him at that hour containing a link to a news report, asking whether it was true, whether it was going to be a problem, and, if so, whether we had a response. Zelenskyy read a lot of the news himself, in local publications and on social media. In fact, his inner circle, people like his chief of staff and secretary, joked about removing some of his phone apps so he would be less distracted.

One thing Zelenskyy did every day, everywhere he went, almost without exception was exercise. He would hop on the treadmill or work out in his gym at home; on his first diplomatic trip to Brussels, he was even interviewed on an exercise bike. There was a time when he recorded video messages on his treadmill. In Donbas one morning in 2021, he posted a selfie on Instagram in front of some shabby bars with a brief caption sharing his location: "Avdiivka. Promka. Bars. Good Morning!" Most likely, Zelenskyy was out taking a morning jog.

Zelenskyy considered sports so important that in June 2020 he promoted the launch of a special initiative called Healthy Ukraine, to encourage people to exercise and have a healthy lifestyle. It was part of a larger government program to improve the health outcomes of Ukrainians and dovetailed with his wife Olena's advocacy for better nutrition programs for Ukrainian schoolchildren.

The new year, 2020, began with a national tragedy. On January 8, we received news that a Ukrainian plane had been shot down in Iran. The press office worked overtime to keep people informed about the tragedy. During that period, I personally returned home at 6:30 a.m. one day, going right back to work just hours later by 9:30 a.m. But it was not the endless work that drained me; it was the constant reminder of those innocent victims: 167 passengers and nine crew members shot down by two missiles at 6:14 a.m. Iranian time on January 8. There were no survivors.

Later that month, Zelenskyy, one of the few heads of state with Jewish roots outside Israel, went to that country to meet Prime Minister Benjamin Netanyahu and was scheduled to attend a Holocaust remembrance event at Yad Vashem on Mount Herzl in Jerusalem. Both Putin and Zelenskyy were invited, but only Putin had been asked to speak. When Zelenskyy learned this, he decided to forgo the ceremony and gave his tickets to Holocaust victims.

He was very touched, however, when a group of rabbis invited him instead to Jerusalem's Old City to pray for peace at the Western Wall (Wailing Wall) by the holiest site in Judaism. It clearly meant a lot to him, and he was honored by their welcome. Afterward, he insisted that our press release about the event should include the name of every rabbi who invited him. Zelenskyy rarely, if ever, spoke publicly about his religion. I think it was his way of showing that religion was a purely personal matter, not to be played for political gain. In Ukraine, there are many religions, though Christianity has the largest number of adherents. By not making a big show about his own faith and never supporting one group over the others, Zelenskyy tried to highlight his country's acceptance of all religions.

Soon after his return from his trip to Israel, news of the deadly coronavirus disease arrived in Ukraine, prompting the so-called Novi Sanzhary incident. At the beginning of February 2020, Ukraine equipped a resort in the village of Novi Sanzhary—a settlement in central Ukraine of about eight thousand people—to quarantine several dozen Ukrainian citizens who had returned from China. Frightened by the news of the unknown virus and by disinformation about supposed attempts to exterminate Ukrainians, local inhabitants aggressively protested against the government's initiative. Armed with whatever was at hand, men and women went out to meet the arriving evacuees. Cobblestones—along with hateful insults—were hurled at them as they arrived in a bus. The pictures shocked the world and brought Ukraine into shameful focus.

Prime Minister Honcharuk arrived at the scene of the conflict. He clearly didn't know what to do. Prior to his arrival, the situation had been handled by law enforcement personnel and

Minister of Internal Affairs Arsen Avakov, who was in his seventh year on the job. The prime minister arranged a meeting on camera, at which he picked up a pen and could be seen taking notes while reports were read aloud. This was staged to give the impression that he was in control. But he did not look the law enforcement personnel in the eye or ask anything during their reports. The video of the scene made a memorable impression of an out-of-touch, clueless prime minister.

Later, President Zelenskyy asked the minister of health at the time, Zoryana Skaletska, if she would quarantine herself in the resort for two weeks with the returnees from China, and she agreed to do it. This gesture helped calm the protests somewhat, and after two weeks, Zelenskyy went to greet the group himself. It helped, of course, that after the two-week quarantine, it turned out that none of those evacuees from China had contracted COVID-19.

Shortly after the incident at Novi Sanzhary, Honcharuk behaved in a similar fashion when he was summoned by the president to discuss the rising coronavirus threat and what the government proposed to do about it. During their meeting, in full view of the cameras, Honcharuk again busied himself with taking notes and barely looked up at the president. This absurd posture recalled that of a bright schoolboy who has committed some offense, and it hardly fit the image of the prime minister of Ukraine.

It was quickly becoming apparent in Ukraine—as was the case in many other parts of the world—that the government was woefully unprepared to deal with the pandemic. After the COVID-19 threat had already become painfully clear, our government was unable even to stop the export of masks, which were already being made in Ukraine, to other countries, leaving many Ukrainians unprotected. Honcharuk was proving himself incapable of drawing up a concerted plan to address the crisis.

The lack of tests, masks, and even laboratories for proper analysis was frightening, especially since, as widely acknowledged before the pandemic, the fragile health system in Ukraine not only had been neglected but was rife with corruption.

In the midst of this crisis, after less than a year in office, Andriy Bohdan, the first head of the presidential office—essentially the president's chief of staff, who managed the workflow for the president—left his position, and Andriy Yermak succeeded him. Bohdan's departure was followed soon afterward by Prime Minister Honcharuk's resignation and the appointment of his successor, Denys Shmyhal, and an entire reshuffling of the leadership. At the end of that first year of his presidency, Zelenskyy remarked, "There were no more 'guys just doing their job' on the new team. We all had to be statesmen."

In this endless stream of crises, the resignation of the first government did not seem like a great loss for the country, at least to me. Yet these changes in February and March 2020 caused a storm of negative reaction, especially from Ukraine's international partners. Zelenskyy, unfortunately, chose to remain silent in response. The lack of explanation only made the situation worse. But Zelenskyy had one important rule that may explain his silence: he would never make excuses to anyone. As a political manager, he had yet to learn to walk the line between making excuses and explaining what was happening.

Zelenskyy always said it was hard to lose those he had worked with most closely, the members of his tightly knit team. But despite his loyalty, he had to readjust to political realities. One of

Zelenskyy's biggest problems was the lack of people with the necessary expertise and experience. For the most part, he relied on
his inner circle and their personal contacts to fill positions. But
it was not sufficient.

Honcharuk's exit, particularly, surprised and perturbed many
people. Most people thought that he had been moving successfully
in the direction of reforms and was let go because of an unfortu-
nate leaked recording. In the recording, Honcharuk was heard
speaking condescendingly about President Zelenskyy's knowledge
of economics and critically of the president's manner of governing. "Zelenskyy has a very primitive, that is to say simplistic, understanding of economic processes," Honcharuk's voice was heard to
say. "If the president has no immediate answers to this question,
there will be an empty space there into which any fucking idea can
arrive about the government bond. . . . That stuff comes into his
head only because he is clueless." (What amused me most about
Honcharuk's remarks is that he also had no training in monetary
policy. Several months earlier, he could not explain to me the reasons for inflation, pleading that he was not an economist.)

His tenure ended as quickly as his entry, when he had rid-
den into the government office on a scooter at the beginning of
his premiership. In fact, the reasons for Honcharuk's departure
were much deeper than mere style. First, he had insufficient institutional experience. It's not easy to make the transition from
political activist to prime minister of a country of forty million
people without having any experience in running a governmental bureaucracy. He was noticeably at a loss in critical situations;
he talked a lot but barely understood how the political system
operated.

By the end of March, with COVID-19 raging, the government

decided to impose a national lockdown for the first time, which lasted more than two months. Zelenskyy did not, however, agree to institute a state of emergency, because he wanted to allow time for the farmers to sow their fields. The first lockdown was crucial; it provided the country with an opportunity to hold off the initial tide of infections and to prepare its medical infrastructure. When thousands of coronavirus deaths were being counted every day in the West, Ukrainians were sitting at home, worried about their financial losses. The government was buying personal protective equipment and looking for money from the international community to survive the crisis. But to our credit, we had a fairly low increase in the disease rate until the middle of July 2020.

Every day we gathered the government for online meetings, hearing reports from Prime Minister Shmyhal, the minister of healthcare, law enforcement, and the National Security and Defense Council. Every day, almost desperately, we were looking for ways out of the situation.

Ukrainian villages lacked access to outpatient clinics, and in many cities, there were hospitals that had not been renovated for decades. There was a shortage of basic supplies like bandages and syringes. Doctors worked around the clock, at first even without protection. The authorities seemed powerless. The situation with COVID-19 tests was typical of the deplorable level of preparedness: a person could wait seven to ten days for the results of a test that in turn had a high probability of unreliability. The Ministry of Healthcare never set up a system to collect truthful and reliable statistics because it never had the information on those who recovered. My aunt in the backwoods of Kherson region would not have known what to do if she had suddenly needed an ambulance that barely served her far-flung village.

But there was another, more positive side to this story. At the beginning of the epidemic, Ukraine could do only two hundred tests a day; by summer, we were already doing fifty thousand. By the end of the year, Ukraine had doubled the number of oxygen-supplied beds to fifty-four thousand. And the state resumed doing laboratory work and began building a large new laboratory center to create vaccines for the future.

Despite our successes, COVID-19 instilled a sense of hopelessness across the country, with the economy going into shock. While the government continued to pursue needed reforms—such as a crucial vote in late March to lift the moratorium on buying and selling farmland in Ukraine, which up till then could only be inherited, and a new banking law designed to limit the influence of oligarchs on banks, which finally unlocked much-needed IMF funding—its attempt at a complete overhaul of the country's institutions stalled.

Then, on September 25, 2020, a second major national tragedy occurred. This time, a military transport plane, an AN-26, crashed near Chuhuiv Air Base in Ukraine during a training flight. Of the twenty-seven people aboard twenty-six died: seven instructors and nineteen cadets. President Zelenskyy visited the only survivor, a cadet, and the next day created a commission to investigate the circumstances surrounding the incident. He went on to announce a program of assistance for the families of the victims and declared a day of national mourning, but this catastrophe, in concert with the mounting COVID-19 infections, depressed us even more. We were shaken.

Despite it all, local elections were still slated for October, when mayors, heads of the villages and united territorial communities, and deputies of local councils would be chosen.

The pandemic had become an enormous challenge for regional officials. They bore the brunt of people's anger over restrictions imposed by the national government to reduce the spread of the disease. Local authorities came to realize early on that the risk of incurring their constituents' anger might outweigh those presented by the virus itself. So, after the first spring lockdown, some local authorities began allowing mass events in violation of government regulations. Suddenly, in the midst of the pandemic, concerts became possible in some cities, restaurants kept serving, and nightclubs, discos, and other places of entertainment opened their doors, saving the tourist business.

The mayor of Cherkasy, the administrative center in central Ukraine, tried to campaign on his opposition to Zelenskyy. There were also tensions with the mayors of the eastern megalopolis Dnipro and the southern resort town of Odesa. When Zelenskyy arrived to campaign, he was met by organized protests. The same was true in the western city of Lviv, a popular tourist destination that had supported Zelenskyy's predecessor, Petro Poroshenko.

Local politicians were angry at the new government for not giving them more attention and support, for the fact that the government was new and they were used to the old one, and because the pandemic was still disrupting their lives. None of them were core supporters of Zelenskyy's Servant of the People party, which had won big in the 2019 elections. Their festering, unresolved problems, sometimes tens of years old, stoked anger and opposition, and it didn't help that the new, often very young and inexperienced candidates didn't have much in terms of concrete remedies to offer. Regions revolted and protested, using administrative resources and the media to express their anger, filled with a growing sense of injustice.

The first deputy chief of staff, Serhii Trofimov, in charge of regional policy, had not been effective in his job. He sincerely thought he was doing everything possible to solve the problems. But the problems multiplied. In meetings, every time the COVID-19 numbers in the regions rose again and regions were protesting against government anti-pandemic measures by allowing different mass entertainment events, Zelenskyy turned to his appointee, asking what was going on. Trofimov, a former Kvartal 95 producer and a taciturn man by nature, usually explained himself in two words. "I know," he would say without offering any details. Sometimes he even said less, offering one modest word: "Working."

Zelenskyy himself contracted COVID-19 in mid-November, during a surge in cases in Ukraine. He went into quarantine at Feofania Clinical Hospital in the southern outskirts of Kyiv and had a mild fever, but he did not get much sicker. Expressions of support flooded in from all over the world. In a show of concern, many Jewish rabbis offered prayers of healing. I was sent video recordings of them praying, from Israel, Belgium, France, Dubai, and Ukraine, and forwarded them to the president in the hospital. Normally, Zelenskyy responded to texts only on important political matters, but he responded to all of these.

The results of the regional elections were fascinating. On the one hand, Zelenskyy's party won overall; on the other hand, in the mayoral elections, the incumbents prevailed. Ukrainians were used to trusting the incumbent mayors to such an extent that they did not even think about other candidates.

The most incredible story concerned the mayor of Kharkiv, an eastern city with a million-plus population that would later be devastated and demolished by the Russian invasion in 2022. Hennadii Kernes had won reelection in 2020 for the third time, getting more than 60 percent support, far ahead of all the other candidates, without ever appearing in public, as he was seriously ill. Soon after his victory, Kernes died, posthumously inheriting the title of "ghost mayor." There was no question of a new election. By law, the secretary of the city council took over, and an early election had to be set by the parliament. Experts said that the announcement of a new election for mayor could be postponed for years. Finally, it was scheduled for Halloween 2021.

Although he failed to elect any mayors from his party, President Zelenskyy still emerged the winner overall. Early on, he had viewed the situation pragmatically, having suspected that his party wouldn't be able to oust any of these politically entrenched leaders. As a result, in preelection interviews, he set modest expectations for the mayoral races for his young party and worked on electing other local council officials. And the Servant of the People party prevailed, electing more local council members and other officials than any other party, some six thousand in all.

Why do I say that Zelenskyy was the one who had succeeded and not us? Because that statement is accurate. In fact, all the politicians and near-politicians benefited from the work and popularity of just one person: Zelenskyy. It was no secret. Except that sometimes newly minted politicians thought they had done it on their own. On the whole, though, everyone understood that fact.

"We're all in the same boat. But I gave them the oar they're

rowing with," Zelenskyy said one day. And I can't think of anything clearer than that quote. Even those who were not supporters of Zelenskyy still understood why he became president.
By the end of 2020, there was not a single politician in Ukraine
anywhere close to Zelenskyy in terms of popularity.

CHAPTER 3

Becoming Press Secretary to the President

It is not easy for Ukrainians to write about themselves, and, in fact, in our part of the world it is often considered a sign of narcissism or, worse, an act of political provocation. That is how my post-Soviet generation was brought up for decades, still under the influence of the values of the USSR even though the Soviet Union had long since been dissolved. Personality or individualism had little importance. Ukraine hasn't been an independent state for even half as long as it was a part of the Soviet Union, and not everyone has thought about the psychological import of this fact, at least not yet. Nobody taught us in Ukraine to be an individual, to have a personality, and to be ourselves.

In the United States, students are taught to write personal statements, without which one can't accomplish anything. You can't get into a university or win a contest without writing a personal essay. In fact, most professional applications require written personal statements. You need to describe yourself; list your skills, your abilities, and your suitability for the chosen job; and add some words about your leadership style and your personal and professional strengths.

I remember that the first application letters I wrote seemed like acts of terrible self-promotion. It took me a long time to learn to accept that what I wrote were, in fact, my accomplishments. But to do this, I had to come to terms with a lot of self-doubts that had blossomed in the years I spent in a world of post-Soviet realities.

Many times, I have seen Ukrainians who are often stronger personally or professionally than people from other countries. Yet even if a Ukrainian knows English well enough to take some modern professional course in the United States or EU, he or she often lacks the most important thing: an understanding of how a Westerner thinks and how to assert that he or she is the best candidate for a training position.

We had been closed-minded for so long and we had been taught that the West was bad for so long that some people from the older generation reflexively called the United States "the enemy," which the USSR had taught us to fear. But after the invasion in 2022, even they understood that Russia was the real enemy.

This was the environment in which I grew up. Fear, obedience, monotony—but it was something that I naturally and intuitively could not accept.

I was raised in Kherson, a city in the south of the country with about three hundred thousand people. It is the only region with access to two seas, the Black Sea and the Sea of Azov, and when I was a kid, I was taken in dusty old buses to the beaches.

I will share with you now the most important secret from my

childhood. There, in Kherson, are the tastiest tart cakes one can imagine. They are insanely cheap because they are made in a state enterprise factory and sold mostly in public institutions: hospitals and schools. They are so good, I would recommend visiting the regional hospital, where my mom and dad work, and grabbing five at a time.

In the spring of 2022, I planned to go to Kherson with the intention of feeding these tart cakes to my fiancé, Pavlo, as part of an introduction to my childhood. When I was a child, I once got so sick that I refused to eat anything. Only by accident did my parents find these tarts, and all through my illness they were the only thing I ate.

But in the spring of 2022, the Kherson region was occupied by the Russians. I did not know if I would ever see my parents and relatives again or be able to introduce them to Pavlo.

Cake production stopped, and, without warning, we urgently needed to seek humanitarian aid from abroad, including food and medicine for the city. The Russians would not let anything into Kherson: no medicine, no food, not even baby formula. It was possible to deliver these necessities only by what the Ukrainians call "thieves' ways." This is how we tried to deliver the truckloads of whatever we could. Every day I got reports from my parents about how they were running out of food, how my father was standing in miles-long lines from 6:00 a.m. to get butter. It was something my parents remembered from the time when we were part of the Soviet Union. No one could believe it was happening again.

Pavlo went to the front lines in the region around Kherson to try to do something, to help liberate the city. I joked, "Is your desire to meet your mother-in-law that strong?"

He replied, "I want to give you back your hometown as a wedding present."

We laughed and cried at the same time. War is full of pain.

———

Kherson was where I learned my first words, it was the place where I stood up for the Ukrainian language. It was there that I was taught to work hard if I wanted to achieve something.

I remember having a good childhood, though I had few friends and suffered from low self-esteem because I was the only child at school who spoke Ukrainian as my native language; I didn't even understand Russian at first. I remember spending the last three years of school in an endless cycle of study and increasingly more difficult competitive examinations on Ukrainian language and literature. Later, those victories helped me get into university.

I also studied English. I remember the dark, snowy evenings when my mother and I walked over to the teachers' lounge at school for my private lessons. Wrapped in a scarf, I warmed my frozen nose with my breath and constantly complained about the long walk to meet the English teacher. My mother gave all the money she had for these lessons—in the early 1990s, they cost an unbelievable amount: $5 an hour. But they lasted an hour and a half, which I really did not like as a kid. My teacher thought I was talented and tried to give me some extra time. There were moments when we ran out of money, so my mother bartered or went into debt so I could continue to study. Only now as an adult do I realize how much importance my parents placed on my English studies. I think my mother believed in her heart that it would give me the opportunity to marry a foreigner.

Despite our very limited means, I went to the best university in the country. Higher education in Ukraine is still mostly free. Thanks to my high scores on multiple competitive exams and my comparatively high level of English, I managed to get accepted. And eight years later, I successfully defended my doctoral thesis on modern Ukrainian poetry.

It is difficult for me to assess the impact of all those years of study on my formation as a professional. But I read Kant and Nietzsche with great interest, and through a lot of independent reading, I learned much more about life than from bibliographies of outdated literature or conversations with professors, many of whom had drowned their consciences in a glass or two of local cognac.

During my doctoral studies, I applied to attend an academic conference at Charles University in Prague, in the Czech Republic, and was invited to take part. I had never been outside Ukrainian borders in my life. Everything in my life at the time argued against taking the trip.

For one thing, the cost of traveling amounted to almost all my savings. Because I was officially registered to live in Kherson, my hometown, I had to go to the eastern city of Donetsk (about a five-hundred-mile journey) to get a visa, even though I was living in Kyiv at the time, where the Czech Republic had a consulate. Furthermore, my parents were afraid that if I attended the conference, I would disappear in Europe.

I remember my enthusiasm and almost childlike delight when I received the conference invitation. I was thrilled to be able to tell my professor about it. He smiled through his mustache, then brushed me off like an annoying fly: Get out of here, he said.

That did not make any sense to me. I thought that a talk at one of Europe's most famous and respected universities and publication of an academic paper in a peer-reviewed journal should count for something. But seemingly not for my Ukrainian professor. Post-Soviet rules dictated a different logic: according to these, only publication in a Ukrainian university academic journal registered by the Higher Attestation Commission (HAC) was considered valuable.

"I'll publish it at Charles University!" I said, and prepared for the conference. My department, however, viewed the conference as little more than a secondary school field trip. But I learned my lesson. By the time I completed my graduate studies, I had three times as many papers published by HAC-approved universities than the rules required. And I never went to another academic conference abroad in my field of study.

It was only later, in my last year of graduate school in 2012, that I learned about the widespread practice of bribery in the Ukrainian education system. I had never paid a bribe to anyone until it was time to defend my doctoral dissertation. When I complained that my professor had refused to touch my thesis for more than three weeks and the deadline was fast approaching, his department colleagues explained to me that I was required to give him a bribe.

Then I watched as my esteemed professor of modern Ukrainian literature thumbed through the pages. My face turned red with shame, but I'll never forget what he said when he found what he was looking for: "Now I see it. Your work is good." As it turned out, I discovered later, my humiliating experience submitting my dissertation in the best university in Ukraine, Taras

Shevchenko National University of Kyiv, an institution recognized throughout the world, was by no means unique, as I'll explain later in this chapter. For this and other reasons, after I got my Ph.D. in 2012, I decided not to pursue an academic career.

———

To cover living expenses while in graduate school, I took a job at one of Ukraine's largest TV channels. Starting as a morning copy editor, I slowly worked my way up to become a half-decent correspondent. I still think of that news show as my real alma mater. I faced no censorship and was grateful for all the support that the cozy newsroom gave me. I willingly spent months without days off. I really wanted to learn how to be a TV journalist. When people asked me why I chose to work in that field, I knew the answer: as a child, I often heard from my grandmother that the smartest people work on TV.

———

After the 2014 Revolution of Dignity, Ukraine began to change. To the old, unhealed post-Soviet traumas, new ones were added. The Russian Federation violated past treaties, forcibly annexing the Ukrainian peninsula of Crimea and then invading part of eastern Ukraine, the area known as Donbas. It was not only the loss of territories that was unsettling, but the invasion brought continual war to the eastern part of our country, with all its attendant evils: the wounding or death of loved ones, displacement, destruction and endless grief for millions of families, and crippled fates. Sorrow and despair settled over us. But at the same time, these shared traumas galvanized us all in Ukraine, allowing us to cope with the attacks, stop some of them, and defend our country. The war changed us, revealing our ideals and talents.

I, too, realized I had to expand my horizons. During the revolution in 2014, when I had the opportunity to work with an American journalist for an international TV channel, I noticed how different Western journalism was from the cozy domestic reporting inside Ukraine. I started studying American newspapers and seeing what they wrote about Ukraine. Then I went to Moldova to study the experience of the European-style reforms that had swept through that country. Moldova had its own "Donbas," called Transnistria, where Russia had started a similar military conflict using the same hybrid warfare, turning part of Moldova into a gray zone in the center of Europe. A TV cameraman and I went there illegally and were struck by the desolation and the number of KGB officers.

Then, in the same year, 2014, I won a place in the journalism program named after the former Polish president Lech Wałęsa. It wasn't solely due to my academic credentials: the West had become more interested in Ukrainians after the Revolution of Dignity. In any case, I had the opportunity to spend two weeks in Gdańsk, where the first Polish trade union, Solidarity, headed by Wałęsa, had started the struggle for Polish independence at the end of the 1980s. It was the first chance I had to appreciate the experience of journalists from many countries; also, it was a chance to improve my English. I realized how many things I still had to learn to become a good journalist.

While in the program, I managed to do a short, but very serious, exclusive interview with Wałęsa for the Ukrainian TV channel I was working for. Wałęsa had some extremely important words for Ukraine: about his support for us, about the fact that we should not give up, that our revolution meant a lot to the world. Most important, he was grateful that Ukraine had stopped the terrible Russian invasion of Donbas in 2014. I don't know about the rest of Poland, but at the end of 2014, Poles in Gdańsk viewed Ukraine as a heroic country. When we met them on the streets, even the ordinary shipyard workers shook our hands as a gesture of heartfelt support across national boundaries.

That was the last trip I took for the TV channel where I had been working for six and a half years. Although my bosses had been very good to me, I knew that the best they could offer would no longer be enough. I knew it was time to move on. Between 2014 and 2017, I worked for several different TV channels, slowly climbing up the career ladder.

I had never been really interested in any career for its own sake. I simply tried to do the best I could in each job I had, taking every opportunity to learn as much as possible. My bosses seemed to appreciate that. Still, I changed jobs quite a few times from 2014 to 2019. It wasn't that I couldn't stay in one place, but I was looking for a job that fulfilled me the most and that would be the best fit, both in terms of values and working environment.

Still, there were challenges. I first hosted a small investigative show for six months on a new TV channel that was supposedly independent. But to my surprise I faced censorship and primitive "counterpropaganda" from the channel, which was owned by a member of the political party of Ukraine's then president Poroshenko. Then I got lucky again. Somehow, I managed to land one of the best fellowships in my life. The World Press Institute, a prestigious institution based in Saint Paul, Minnesota, established in 1961, offered a nine-week program of study and travel in the United States. I was the first Ukrainian journalist to receive a fellowship. The program had been accepting one person each year from post-Soviet countries, and it had almost always been a Russian. But, again, in part because of the considerable interest in Ukraine at that time, I was chosen from among fourteen Ukrainian candidates.

The program brought ten international journalists at a time to the United States and took them on a tour of eleven states, visiting the most prominent newsrooms, civil organizations, and state agencies. I visited the White House and the UN General Assembly. I toured the headquarters of the *New York Times*, the *Washington Post*, the *Wall Street Journal, Politico*, the *Los Angeles Times*, and many other publications. It was then that I also became acquainted with the Black Lives Matter movement, which I reported on as a journalist less than a year later. During my time in the States, I also did freelance work on air from the UN General Assembly in New York City for another new Ukrainian TV channel: eleven broadcasts in two and a half days. I remember that trip well. Back in 2016 it was still very exciting.

After I returned to Ukraine, I was offered a full-time position at that same new TV channel to cover the European Union in Brussels. Frankly speaking, it was not a great option: it paid poorly (about $500 a month), and I did not see much opportunity for advancement. But I needed a job, and working for an independent, uncensored TV channel with cutting-edge technology was the best choice I had, so I took it. We did live broadcasts from our phones and carried the equipment for them in little blue backpacks.

I had been at that channel for only a few months, but with eight years of experience already under my belt, I soon began to feel like a professional "old lady" there. And, in fact, I never managed to get to Brussels, because first I had an urgent surgery, then I broke my leg. It was as if fate was telling me this was not a good match for me. Besides, after the World Press Institute program, I found it difficult to return to the narrow confines of national political journalism and local news, such as coverage of snow removal or debunking a supposed ban on checking bus drivers for alcohol. So I decided to try freelancing in my spare time for foreign media.

Even before I returned to Ukraine, I had already pitched some ideas to foreign media outlets. One of them, about the post-traumatic stress disorder afflicting Ukrainian war veterans in Donbas, was picked up by Vice News. Subsequently the Vice News team and I made a documentary about the consequences of the war in Donbas and how it affected every resident who fought there or fled from there. It was distributed worldwide and got a fair amount of attention.

After that, I published a story stemming from my own experiences with corruption in Ukrainian universities. I had told a professor I met in the United States about how the dissertation payment system worked and how this corruption was killing our education. He listened and asked, "Why don't you talk about it? You're a journalist!"

I had no answer to such a simple and logical question. I had, in fact, tried to write about this in 2012, when I was still a graduate student, but Viktor Yanukovych, the most corrupt president of Ukraine, was in power then, and I didn't have any success. After the 2014 Revolution of Dignity, Yanukovych went into exile in Russia, and his house was turned into a museum of corruption.

But it was 2016 now and times were different. An anti-corruption campaign, designed together with the help of Western institutions, was gaining steam in Ukraine. The Yanukovych mafia had left the country, and everyone could breathe more easily. Each of us had to do something to build the country we wanted to live in. "Everyone knows that Ukrainian education is corrupt," the professor said to me. "But no one knows how this corruption works. This story will be of interest to the world."

The article took about two months to research, and I uncovered some interesting stuff. While tuition costs for higher education were very democratic in Ukraine—averaging less than $1,000 per academic year—paying bribes was commonplace. A student from Mariupol in eastern Ukraine told me that she spent an unimaginable amount of money on bribes during the four years she spent writing her Ph.D. thesis. She paid her adviser $1,000 to thank him for his mentoring. The same sum went to another professor for editing her papers, even though this was part of his regular duties. And this was the fate of nearly every Ukrainian student: Victoria, a student at my university's journalism institute, knew she wouldn't pass her junior-year exam without paying her professor $300. Katya, in the medical program, skimped on food to afford $50 for every grade during the semester. A few male students from Kharkiv knew they could simply pay for their diplomas, so they skipped the exams altogether.

In reporting the story, I went back to my alma mater without a student ID, and with some old-school cunning and sweet talk, I managed to slip by the guards and walk the familiar university halls. On the walls were framed portraits of the university's professors, most of whom I knew from my dissertation defense, in the style of North Korean party officials. Almost every university worker was a relative or a friend of someone in a position of at least some authority. Once, the head of my institute agreed to employ a woman who had recently had a child and didn't want to work, but still wanted a paycheck. It was a favor between friends.

To understand the magnitude of this problem, you had to understand the size of Ukraine's educational system. It was too gigantic to thrive by legal means. In 2016, there were 664 higher education institutions in Ukraine—260 more universities than in Germany, even though Ukraine's population was half the size of Germany's. This figure did not include the 139 universities that the Ministry of Education and Science (MES) had closed a year earlier because of license discrepancies. It was hard to imagine that anyone could be successful in changing the system until the ruling educator-godfathers were replaced. But they would be unseated only when bribes, a major source of their revenue, were stopped.

Robert Orttung, an expert at George Washington University on post-Soviet systems of corruption, spent two months traveling around Ukraine with a team of researchers and asked regular people where they most frequently encountered corruption. He told me that education ranked third on the list, after the medical system and the police. "The main reason for education's prominence as an area of corruption is that often professors and teachers receive small salaries so they have a need for more income," Orttung wrote in an email to me. "They have to extract money where they can in order to survive, and that basically amounts to demanding bribes. . . . Everyone would be better off if the system could be made more formal and transparent, so that instead of paying bribes, people [would] pay taxes and the state could fund services," Orttung added. "Of course, few want to pay taxes because they do not trust the state to provide good services."

But the fight against corruption in universities after the revolution was so slow that it seemed as if curtailing bribery in higher education was not in fact a government priority. The MES organized lectures on civil responsibility and required that professors create special anti-corruption committees to police their own departments. The results spoke for themselves: in 2016, the MES learned about only one corrupt academic. A senior lecturer was accused of taking a $100 bribe. He received a two-year probation.

My article was published in *Politico Europe*. For about twenty-four hours after the piece appeared, I felt like I couldn't breathe. I had just shared one of my most painful experiences with the world. In response to the piece, I received hundreds of messages of support and gratitude and even a few threats.

The matter didn't stop there. The story I wrote was picked up by national media in Ukraine and debated in the MES. Deputies in parliament requested an investigation be conducted, and my university was forced to respond to the piece. The university then manufactured a lawsuit designed to portray my case as an isolated dispute between a former student and a teacher. My professor was told that if he didn't agree to sue to "recover his honor and dignity," he would be fired. So he sued. According to court documents, he asked for $120: $80 to recover his court costs, with the remaining $40 the amount he placed on his honor and dignity. He initially won his case, but I appealed, and the verdict was eventually overturned—four and a half years later. I was proud that I had fought this and won, because each of us should fight for our values any way we can.

———

By then, I was in a rut at my TV job. It felt very wrong for me. I started thinking hard about what I really wanted to do. I was almost thirty, and television seemed like a fun game but nothing more. So I did what any millennial would do: I got a tattoo and then I quit my job at the TV channel.

Only after that did I get serious.

I developed a résumé in English and applied for several international jobs in Kyiv and for a short journalism training program at Yale University. Despite previous trips abroad, I was still very worried about my English. Yes, it was better than in 2014, but it still was not professional enough. So, I started reading English texts out loud, talked to foreign friends, and tried to answer my own questions in front of a mirror.

This was the time when I took some major steps in my career. I realized then that I had to decide what I wanted to do, invest in myself, and make some wise choices. I knew I should have pursued these goals earlier but I'd thought I could learn on the job.

I applied and was accepted to Thread, Yale University's four-day storytelling workshop for professional journalists in various media, including print, video, podcasting, photography, and other hybrid forms, sponsored by the Yale Journalism Initiative. Unfortunately, it did not offer a scholarship. Few people in the United States would believe that an international journalist would have trouble finding a couple thousand dollars to pay for the tuition, but for me it wasn't so easy. I had about $3,000 left in my savings, including some cash I got from selling my car. That was how much it cost to pay for the course, a ticket to the United States, and a few days' stay there.

I didn't know what to do. I sat for a long time with my fingers over the keyboard: if I pressed the button and paid for the course, there would be no going back. All the laws of logic were against it, and so were my family and friends. A newly unemployed person spending her savings on a course of study might seem crazy. I was aware of that.

But there were some other factors that seemed important for me to consider. I was an adult with friends and contacts, with a lot of experience and an established reputation. In the worst case, I could always return to my last TV job, but could I get accepted to that same course the next time? With a push of a button, I killed all my "Soviet" fears and trusted the universe. The course didn't start for a few weeks. During that time, the world could turn upside down. And it did.

———

Before I left for the storytelling course at Yale, I was offered a job at the International Committee of the Red Cross (ICRC). Preparing for my job interview, I had studied its entire website and its terminology, read Wikipedia articles, and familiarized myself with the international laws under which the ICRC works. The top communications manager had praised my English, and the other staff members seemed friendly and welcoming. The opportunity to work with an international team on projects helping civilians in a military environment gave me a sense of greater fulfillment. But I couldn't bring myself to sign the contract at a Friday meeting, and we rescheduled for Monday.

As I left the Red Cross offices that Friday and headed into the subway toward home, I got a Facebook message from a woman I didn't know. She introduced herself as the head of the international department of one of the largest Ukrainian TV channels and offered me a job as an international correspondent. It was actually hard to believe that this channel didn't yet have a journalist to cover Donald Trump's and Hillary Clinton's presidential campaigns, but it turned out to be true. I met with the head of the network on Saturday and accepted the job on Sunday. I ended up spending a month and a half in the United States, finding a place to stay in the Pentagon City area and traveling to New York, Ohio, and Philadelphia to cover political events. In September, I returned to Kyiv to work at the TV station.

The day after my thirtieth birthday, just days after I returned to work, the TV network's building was set on fire, and our international department burned to the ground. My colleague Liuda, a twenty-two-year-old woman from western Ukraine known for her patriotism, was preparing a text about the G20 summit when about twenty men in military-looking uniforms burst through the channel's front door. They had brought tires, the symbol of the Revolution of Dignity, which groups of far-right nationalists and provocateurs were now using for various purposes, mostly to discredit revolutionary values on Russian TV channels and to paint a picture of a radical, violent Ukraine. Perhaps their goal was to make the Ukrainian capital look as if it were under siege in order to discredit the government's leaders, who had proclaimed their desire for European values and requested entry into the EU.

I had just arrived for the evening shift. Both Liuda and I did not take the group's entry into the building seriously at first. I filmed the men for a few seconds—as a memento—and called the editor to say that the text Liuda had been working on was ready. In response, I heard a shout: "Close the windows and doors!" And the editor hung up.

It was only then that I realized the men had actually broken into the building. I went out into the hallway. It was smoky, and there were two guys in respirators coming down the stairs, yelling, "Fire! Run!" It wasn't until late that night, after talking to my coworkers, that I remembered those guys didn't have fire-fighting uniforms. They were the arsonists.

It took us a few seconds to grab our bags and run down the stairs. That's when I completely panicked: the same guys in military-looking uniforms were blocking the entrance, and the building was filling with smoke. It quickly occurred to me that if the guys could set fire to a building with people inside, they could also attack us physically. But that feeling lasted only a few seconds: we were allowed to leave. About fifteen minutes later, the arsonists also left the building, which was on fire. Thick smoke from burning tires rose to the sky.

Outside, the arsonists put on a little show: a girl with a bouquet of flowers, symbolizing Ukraine, was embraced by a guy dressed as a heroic Ukrainian Cossack from the Renaissance. I still don't understand what that performance was supposed to mean.

Then, with the flames already visible through the windows, the Cossack began pacing back and forth, smiling and smoking his pipe. One could guess that he really considered himself a patriotic hero fighting the Russian empire. But it was more likely that he belonged to a group of thugs who made money from these kinds of stunts. At that point, people who were still inside began breaking the windows and shouting, "There are people here! Let us out!"

There were about seventy people in the building at the time of the fire, twenty-five of whom were forced to flee to the roof and were eventually rescued. One journalist injured her back while escaping the blaze, five suffered carbon monoxide poisoning, and several barely survived. Almost everyone suffered trauma of some kind. The estimated damage to the TV studio was $430,000.

The attack was never publicly investigated, and the six suspects who were apprehended and accused of setting the building on fire were released. It was the journalists, editors, and filmmakers, and the image of Ukraine that suffered the most. Looking back on this event now, I think it was part of a political game. I can easily imagine how exhausted ordinary Ukrainians were not only by the Kremlin propaganda, the occupation of Crimea, and the war in the east, but also by the continued attempts of domestic politicians to present Ukrainians as a savage, uncivilized tribe, cynically and brutally exterminating one another.

I worked at the channel for a few more months, covering elections in different countries. In December, it sent me to Brussels as a replacement for another correspondent. "If you want to make God laugh, tell him your plans," I thought as I got into the car on my way to the airport. Even though I had not been able to make it to Brussels as a foreign correspondent for one TV channel at the beginning of the year, here I was, going to the heart of the European Union as a journalist for a different channel at the end of the year.

While I was on my way to Brussels, another scandal erupted—this time of a sexual nature. A man I didn't know sent me an obscene message on Facebook. I was outraged and humiliated. On his Facebook page he played the role of a patriotic activist and loving husband and father. His behavior was disgusting. I took a screenshot and posted it on my page, joking that since he thought it was okay to write such things to an unknown woman, it would probably be okay to make it public, too.

I wasn't expecting thousands of reposts and heated discussions. But I'm glad it happened. It showed that Ukrainian society was ready to talk about this in the open. In my opinion, the more developed a country is, the more openly sexism and gender inequality are discussed. People argued and talked, talked and argued again. I was asked in messages what I thought about their comments and about other participants. Some wrote words of support, although I also received a number of unpleasant messages. In addition, other women to whom the man had written similar sexual comments spoke up. It was a first, small #MeToo incident in Ukraine even before there was #MeToo.

For me, the year 2016 was rich in lessons. I was finally able to recognize my talents and the value of my past experiences. On the last day of the year, Carl Hanlon, the head of communications for Europe and Central Asia at the World Bank, called me. Earlier I had applied for a job as a communications consultant engaged in digital and diplomatic communication regarding structural reforms in Ukraine, such as pension, medical, land, and anti-corruption reform. Now he told me he was ready to make me a consultant. It was a message I had been waiting for since October, after four rounds of interviews. I was also waiting to see if the *New York Times*, with which I had been negotiating, would get back to me. I would spend the next two and a half years working as a consultant for the World Bank and freelancing for the *Times*. It was a very rewarding period of my life, and I learned a lot.

I was able to contribute to a number of stories in the *New York Times*, including a few on some pretty explosive topics. For example, a March 20, 2017, article had this headline: "Paul Manafort,

Former Trump Campaign Chief, Faces New Allegations in Ukraine." And then July 15, 2017: "Huge Manafort Payment Reflects Murky Ukraine Politics." One of my favorites appeared in the paper of record on September 15, 2018: "How a Ukrainian Hairdresser Became a Front for Paul Manafort." And then there was a May 1, 2019, story that reported on the potential conflicts of interest between Joe Biden, when he was vice president, and his son Hunter Biden, who served on the board of a Ukrainian energy company ("Biden Faces Conflict of Interest Questions That Are Being Promoted by Trump and Allies"). My stories were not, however, confined just to politics. Among other topics, I reported on sexual abuse in the Ukrainian army, on how hand grenades stolen from the war in Donbas were being increasingly used in domestic crimes, and on a memorial service commemorating the Holodomor, the horrific Ukrainian famine of 1933.

At the end of that time, though, I was ready for something new. On May 3, 2019, at the end of the day, on the spur of the moment, I decided to apply for the job of press secretary for the newly elected president of Ukraine. Everyone was talking about the competition for the job, which Zelenskyy had announced himself in a video on his Facebook page. Colleagues from the World Bank had convinced me that it would be a great job for me. But given Ukraine's history, I doubted that the competition for the job of press secretary would be open and fair. So, with a healthy dose of skepticism, I applied.

I sent off my résumé Friday evening, only to learn from the news later that night that about three thousand candidates had applied. Of course, I had expected that there would be many, *but not that many*, people wanting to work for Zelenskyy. I smiled and decided it was best to forget about getting a response.

Imagine my surprise when a human resources company, a headhunter, called me the next day, on Saturday afternoon, and questioned me about my qualifications, my vision for the country, my motivation, and my willingness to work around the clock. Of course, I said I was prepared to work around the clock and to share my knowledge with a new team. So I made it into the next round, where I had to prepare a text and video with greetings to Ukrainians for May 8, the Time of Remembrance and Reconciliation for Those Who Lost Their Lives during the Second World War, an official UN holiday celebrated in Europe. For about a month, I heard nothing and did not know whether I had done a good job. Mentally I said goodbye to the job opening. But then the HR consultants got back in touch with me. After Zelenskyy's inauguration on May 20, 2019, I was invited for a personal conversation with the president.

It was only then that I finally told my parents that I had applied for the job. I boasted to my mother that the president of our country was coming to his office on a Saturday in order to converse with me, a Ukrainian journalist from Kherson. Never in my life would I have believed that such a thing could happen. I remember saying, "I have a chance, since I got pretty far. But if they don't hire me, I will definitely write in my diary that the president of Ukraine came to work on a Saturday to interview me."

About seven or eight people, including the president, subjected me to a stress test, playing the roles of media sharks. I had to respond to them as a press secretary would. My interlocutors tested my knowledge of current events and of what was going on in the country, my steadiness under fire, and my position on many issues. Then the president, raised as a Russian speaker, spoke with me in Ukrainian and tested my English as well.

I remember clearly that Zelenskyy liked my answer to his question about my motivation: "If someone in this country, even someone from a modest background, can become president, and a girl also from a family with limited means, and from a different region, can win the competition to become his press secretary, then this is a vivid example that the social elevators are working in Ukraine. And what is this if not the Ukrainian dream that we can make happen together?"

I was hired. Over the next several days, I was introduced to members of the team. My appointment to the job was announced on June 3. Rumors had been circulating on social media for a week that I would become Zelenskyy's press secretary. Some journalists tried to confirm it by getting an official comment, especially those who had wanted the position themselves. But the team decided that it was unnecessary to tell anyone before I appeared at my first press briefing. So, without much fanfare, I faced for the first time dozens of cameras, hundreds of journalists, and a lot of questions. For the first time I felt like every word I said turned into national news. The journalists' initial impressions were mostly positive. Someone, however, created a Wikipedia page for me with distorted facts. Sometime later, I also read a few of the many other articles that had been written about me in the media. My favorite was "Zelenskyy's Press Secretary: I Also Used to Be a 'Kremlin Agent.'"

CHAPTER 4

The President's Team

It is very difficult for me to part with people, very difficult.

—VOLODYMYR ZELENSKYY (INTERVIEW, INTERFAX-UKRAINE,

FEBRUARY 11, 2020)

There are two kinds of people in politics: those who support you in power, and those who support you because you are in power. There are far more of the second type, judging from my experience. Probably every political system contains more officials fascinated with the power of their positions than those committed to serving the people.

Zelenskyy's personnel issues were one of the biggest problems he faced in running his government. In fact, he simply did not have enough people to deal with public administration. Like many leaders entering office, he brought with him the people he trusted, who had gone through his successful election campaign with him. Of course, many of them were the same partners with whom he had started Kvartal 95 decades before, the lawyers, producers, and accountants who had helped him build a private comedy empire. Some members of Kvartal 95's press staff worked in the president's communications department. All told, journalists and observers of Zelenskyy's government counted more than thirty people who used to have some kind of position in Kvartal 95 who later became members of parliament, representatives of the President's Office, or heads of departments, including the Security Service of Ukraine.

Zelenskyy was concerned and a bit upset about the revelations that he had brought people from his business into power and was therefore accused of cronyism. But finding enough good people was a challenge, partly because Zelenskyy swept into government with such overwhelming popular support. HR companies couldn't handle the recruitment of so many new people. Zelenskyy had expected his party to win about eighty seats in parliament out of 450. A possible coalition with new faces was thought out in advance, in order to avoid politics as usual with the old guard. But the Ukrainian people wanted change so much that they gave Zelenskyy's new Servant of the People party 254 parliamentary seats; his team could not have imagined this even in the best of scenarios. There were only a limited number of people with some prior political experience to fill all these seats: those who had already served in nonpolitical positions in previous governments, technocrats who were designing reforms, regional politicians, businessmen, and journalists.

But that still left another 154 seats to fill. And that is why photographers, party hosts, and creative industry types recruited from Zelenskyy's entertainment world became members of parliament, entering as members from the Servant of the People party list. This parliament in general had more women than any previous one: every fifth member was female. As Servant of the People had the most seats, this party also brought in the most women: fifty-four in all. (But actually, in percentage terms, Servant of the People did not have the biggest share of women: only 21 percent, compared with 45 percent of the new political party Holos and 37.2 percent of European Solidarity, the party of previous president Petro Poroshenko.)

This vivid performance of democracy brought to power true representatives of the people, who began to quickly change the country and showed the new face of Ukrainian politics. But the political reality turned out to be far more complicated than it had been in the *Servant of the People* TV series, when President Zelenskyy-Holoborodko and his team of friends did such a good job running a fictional country.

These novice parliamentary members had to learn not only how to govern and how to adapt laws that still included a lot of outdated Soviet regulations, but also how to win political games. They made many mistakes and were savaged by the media. They were the targets of distrust and misunderstanding, and they were preyed on by outside political forces; the oligarchs tried to co-opt them and erode Zelenskyy's majority so that the Servant of the People party would have to form a coalition with another faction, in order to make it more difficult to implement the president's initiatives. Their lack of political experience was painfully evident.

But despite the inevitable missteps after coming to power, the new political machine began to work: many reforms were voted on—more than 150 bills in the first months. The bills kept coming, and the Servant of the People party was clearly emerging as a new political force that could not be ignored. But it was also a tumultuous time. The Servant of the People faction in parliament even had to expel some of its members for engaging in political intrigue or because they had aligned themselves with the old political elite.

The most notable among them was MP Oleksandr Dubinskyy. This expulsion was a very significant step. Ever since the Ukrainian elections in 2019, Dubinskyy had worked to undermine the president and his party and had spread conspiracy theories about the International Monetary Fund (IMF), which put the government in a difficult position, as it depended on IMF funding. Although Dubinskyy had joined the Servant of the People faction, he was close to oligarch Ihor Kolomoyskyy, who was beginning to reassert his influence in Ukrainian politics. Among other things, Kolomoyskyy seemed to disagree with the pro-European direction the country was taking.

The final straw came when Dubinskyy was sanctioned by the United States in January 2021 for suspected meddling in the U.S. elections along with another man, Andriy Derkach. Dubinskyy had attended meetings that Derkach had arranged with Rudy Giuliani, President Trump's envoy. Giuliani was known for his attempt to influence the 2020 U.S. presidential election by compelling the Ukrainian government to announce that it was investigating the son of Joe Biden for his relationship with Burisma, a Ukrainian energy company.

When the U.S. sanctions were announced, Zelenskyy asked Dubinskyy to voluntarily leave the party. When he refused, the parliamentary faction voted by a majority to expel him. By having this showdown with Dubinskyy, a powerful political figure because of his closeness to Kolomoyskyy, Zelenskyy and the Servant of the People faction made clear that they would not tolerate this kind of meddling in government affairs. It was a brave thing to do, and it reassured the international community that it was no longer the old style of politics as usual in Ukraine.

I breathed a sigh of relief after Dubinskyy's expulsion because I saw that this man was not helping to strengthen the state of Ukraine. Most likely, though, he had simply been a passive actor, doing someone else's bidding when he spread conspiracy theories about the IMF or met with Giuliani. He gave the impression that, for him, politics was not a public trust but a position that could be used to pursue a client's agenda. This was often the way Ukrainian politicians could earn a handsome living on the side, since fulfilling those sorts of "requests" from influential business groups was very lucrative.

In many ways, the relationships Zelenskyy built within his political team were reminiscent of the relationships he had developed with the Kvartal 95 team when they were producing the TV series *Servant of the People*. Zelenskyy looked for people who were honest and loyal and who had a desire to make the country better. But real-life politics was far more complicated than those on a TV show, managing politicians was more difficult than directing actors, and the scripts often did not develop the way Zelenskyy wanted them to. Politics depended on the human factor even more than on a film set. And there was not the same level of obedience to the director.

After he became president, Zelenskyy quickly saw the extent of the hypocrisy in Ukrainian politics and witnessed how people used their political positions for personal gain. One day, for instance, officials from the National Anti-Corruption Bureau (NABU) walked into the President's Office. The visit was unexpected, as the bureau did not coordinate with the government when it made arrests. They detained an official who had been in the office long before Zelenskyy came to power. She had promised to get someone a job for $300,000.

Later, some people from the president's team began to get into hot water as well. One Servant of the People MP, Serhii Kuzminykh, who had an excellent reputation, was allegedly caught red-handed by the NABU while taking a bribe of approximately $20,000. This fall from grace was particularly painful for Zelenskyy, as Kuzminykh's brother had heroically defended Ukraine at the beginning of the Russian invasion in Donbas in 2014. Then there was the story about the drunk MP from the president's party who caused a major car accident and then used political connections to hide it. This MP was expelled from the party shortly before the Russian invasion in 2022.

Zelenskyy often caught flak for the statements and initiatives of his political appointees. Some of these people were subsequently fired or forced to resign. The president had no choice but to dismiss those who betrayed his initiatives and ideals or who turned out to be incompetent, but he got no pleasure from doing so. After all, he had worked for decades with a team that had outstanding professional ethics, the one he himself had recruited for Kvartal 95 and with which he had such a successful career.

In this new political reality, however, he could not properly vet each of his team members as he had in the past. So he got upset when he heard all these unpleasant stories. Good character mattered to Zelenskyy. It was the foundation on which he formed his view of people. He was badly upset when people were disloyal or when staffers made missteps in communication and opened themselves up to attacks in the media. These errors often discredited the very brightest members of his team. But he was very forgiving, because he knew that, despite a few exceptions, the majority of his people were strong and loyal. Zelenskyy needed people who were idealists and who believed in Ukraine as much as he did himself.

It is worth noting that not a single member of Zelenskyy's team was spared from these attacks. The more good someone did, the more it seemed he or she was demonized or discredited. This was largely because of the hypercharged media environment and all its resources. Public opinion leaders all had their own audiences on social media and did whatever they could to score points and inflict wounds on the country's leadership. These were really not even attacks aimed at the members of the team. None of us was a visible or valuable enough political target. They were attacking Zelenskyy himself through us, trying to knock him out of action by discrediting his staff.

After the election, many people, of course, were trying to retain or secure a role in the new government with varying levels of success. One who had been in the previous government continued to defend his reputation; another wasn't allowed to participate in the allocation of positions and failed to obtain a job for his friend; yet another complained that his impressive political experience had been ignored. There are many reasons for dissatisfaction in politics. And if you try to overturn an entrenched system like the one in Ukraine, there will be many disgruntled people who will attack you in the media.

Sometimes just having a powerful position is enough to attract criticism. The way the old guard treated Zelenskyy's first chief of staff, Andriy Bohdan, is a good example. When he was

chief of staff of the Office of the President, he had the reputation of being the most detestable person in politics. During the
whole time he was in office, the media were clamoring for his
resignation because of the way he ran the office. He was accused
of committing every political sin and of being a terrible communicator. But as soon as Bohdan left his position, the very same
media that had been demonizing him began to present him in
an entirely different light, somehow even portraying him as a
hero, interviewing him and hanging on his every word.

Despite Bohdan's lack of communication skills that amounted
almost to boorishness, he was a serious professional in the legal
field. He could go up against any political force and even take on
the corrupt courts. It was clear that he was confident about winning, both in his lawsuits and in politics.

Bohdan was succeeded in his job by Andriy Yermak, a law-
yer and movie producer, who was Bohdan's complete opposite.
Yermak never left the president's side, accompanying him everywhere at work, on trips around the country, and on any delegation that was going abroad. Zelenskyy, in fact, made Yermak his
right-hand man, relying on him completely. Initially Yermak dealt
with foreign policy issues as an adviser to President Zelenskyy.
Later, as head of the office, he took on many domestic policy
functions, too, though he also stayed involved in foreign relations. He was in charge of negotiations with Moscow before the
2022 war. But after the brutal Russian invasion in 2022, he no
longer took part in the negotiations. New negotiators were appointed, headed by Davyd Arakhamia, a politician and leader of
Zelenskyy's political faction in parliament. Mykhailo Podoliak,
an adviser to Yermak, but in fact closer to Zelenskyy, participated
actively, and he was the one to achieve a lot of results. In fact, he

was one of the most experienced people on Zelenskyy's team and an example of those who devoted their lives to building the state. But Yermak continued to advise Zelenskyy on strategy and tactics to achieve peace.

If you happened to see the two Andriys together, it would be a study in contrasts. On catching sight of Yermak, Bohdan turned into a loudmouth, barking illogical proposals. Yermak would remain silent, suffused with anger, and though mostly silent, he would be devising further strategic intrigues. In the end, Yermak fought for Bohdan's position and got it.

Zelenskyy brought his personal style and a lot of business methods into politics; in many ways, he managed his team as president in the same manner that he had run Kvartal 95. For one thing, he was a workaholic and was insistent on maximizing efficiency, focused on getting as much done as possible. During official trips abroad, we were chronically short on sleep. The first year, when we did not yet have a streamlined work system, I slept only three or four hours a night. Sometimes we flew to three countries in one day to squeeze in the maximum number of events in the time allotted. Zelenskyy had eight to ten, and sometimes even more, meetings in a day, and even with serious jet lag from time differences, sometimes we would start working as soon as we deplaned. Not everyone could hold up under such a schedule, but it was a refreshing change from earlier administrations, where foreign trips were treated as boondoggles and a weeklong trip involved only a few days of official work. (A friend from the United States indignantly told me that the staff of one former Ukrainian president even had allotted time on the official schedule for a stop at the Apple store to purchase the latest-model iPhone.)

In contrast, Zelenskyy treated these trips very seriously in order to spend a minimum amount of money while achieving the greatest results. And he demanded the same of the other members of his government. He wanted to sign agreements that would bring the greatest benefit to Ukraine, conclude the most essential deals, and meet with the most important political and business stakeholders to defend the interests of our country. He realized that only in that way could Ukraine become a competitive partner deserving of trust and respect.

"I arrive in foreign countries in order to sign basic documents for the country. I am not a political traveler. Politicians will not fly on [the government's] budgeted funds for fun," Zelenskyy said, laying down new regulations for the political elite. Indeed, sometimes politicians or advisers paid for their own flights if their roles were not that important, but they wanted to be part of a delegation to cultivate international contacts.

Zelenskyy drove himself hard, and he was no less demanding of his staff. Not surprisingly, only the most steadfast, hardy, and dynamic ones were able to endure the pressure. Many ministers in Zelenskyy's government were noticeably younger, part of the millennial generation. Thanks to technological progress—computers, smartphones, and the internet—they were accustomed to communicating and interacting with the world 24/7 and enjoyed their work in government, rather than considering it a domain of bureaucracy and political wars.

One Zelenskyy-inspired innovation was the creation of the Ministry of Digital Transformation, and another was starting a department of digitalization in each ministry and governmental institution. Of course, such a new tech infrastructure had to be run by a person from a younger generation. At age twenty-eight, Mykhailo Fedorov became the youngest minister in the history of Ukraine, taking over the Ministry of Digital Transformation and building the whole digital infrastructure of the country.

Observing their approaches, I realized that the young ministers and parliamentarians proved the theory of American journalist Joel Stein, who wrote for *Time* magazine and the *Los Angeles Times*. He explained why many experienced older politicians were leery of millennials: "The information revolution has further empowered individuals by handing them the technology to compete against huge organizations: hackers vs. corporations, bloggers vs. newspapers, terrorists vs. nation-states, YouTube directors vs. studios, app-makers vs. entire industries. Millennials don't need us. That's why we're scared of them," Stein wrote in his much-discussed May 2013 essay for *Time*, "Millennials: The Me Me Me Generation."

This was true in politics as well. Beyond their technological prowess, millennials were quick, good at sizing people up, and, what the old political elite found incomprehensible, sincerely dedicated to the goals of improving the country. They scrupulously and courageously avoided overreaching either politically or legally in getting things done, but they exercised the powers they did have that were appropriate to the times and helped advance their goals. They were told they would forfeit respect if they were to dissolve, digitize, or make transparent the organizations that were known to be corrupt. They were told they would weaken their political positions if they didn't kowtow to political leaders and businessmen. However, they responded by either brushing the old guard aside or directly confronting the dysfunctional and corrupt Ukrainian political machine. They were not in the government merely to sit in Soviet-era leather armchairs and twiddle their thumbs. What they wanted was results.

They understood that one might wait forever for the hide-bound agencies that had done nothing for thirty years to fulfill their responsibility to fight corruption. Since assuming their roles, these millennial politicians had been increasing efficiency and digitizing whatever they could, transferring endless Ukrainian documents into an online database. This reduced the need for everyday people to deal with government bureaucracy, helping people access documents more easily and quickly and thereby reducing corruption. Articles by experts like Carlos Santiso on the Organisation for Economic Co-operation and Development's blog *Development Matters* have advocated the use of digitalization as a tool for fighting corruption: "Digitalisation can disrupt corruption by reducing discretion, increasing transparency, and enabling accountability by dematerialising services and limiting human interactions. Furthermore, it allows for more effective oversight by smarter accountability institutions and data-savvy civil society." These changes were also introduced in the social sphere, in business, and in the legal field. For example, it is now possible to get married online, and registering a new business takes a few hours on the phone instead of having to wait in long lines and run through various agencies for weeks. The young government was moving most of its services to smartphones, as Zelenskyy had envisioned. It was one of the biggest initiatives of his presidency. Digitalization ensured a faster and more effective method of operation and relied on technology and IT. This department became one of the most progressive in the country.

At the end of 2020, digitalization, almost for the first time, demonstrated its enormous value. The new Diia app served as an effective instrument for helping business: through it, more than five hundred thousand entrepreneurs received financial assistance to support their workers during the COVID-19 pandemic. At that time, this was a colossal breakthrough. Registration with Diia and verification of a business took a very short time and could be accomplished just with the help of smartphones, and once completed, people got the financial support. Once in operation, Diia also provided social assistance to people who suffered after the Russian invasion in 2022.

There were other uses for the internet, too. Like many young people, the new ministers and MPs were also easily able to access the endless stream of rumors on social media, the purpose of which, among others, was to stir up trouble among the staff. Some of the older ministers found it difficult to keep up with the constant online chatter, since almost every week they were subjected to new barrages of insults and rumors supposedly emanating from "sources in the Office of the President," saying it was time for them to pack their things and leave.

This undermined the confidence of many, as they started doubting that their work was appreciated or thought they were being sabotaged by their opponents. Many were afraid that the rumor mill meant that they had made enemies who could slander them in front of the president.

Over time, the members of the government realized that those supposed "sources" didn't exist, and they simply carried on with their work. But these endless rumors continued to feed doubts that were discussed over a snifter of cognac every now and then.

Parliament was also subject to the influence of channels on Telegram, an encrypted messaging application produced by a Russian inventor that was popular in post-Soviet space. Overall, this social network succeeded in keeping the entire political army in touch and, accordingly, influenced relations and decisions within the staff to one degree or another. Three Telegram channels were particularly influential among the political elite and earned a lot of money simply on the strength of a rumor that the president was reading them. Businessmen and politicians were paying writers around $1,000 for an absurd one-to-two-hundred-word report in order "to be read by the president" and thus try to influence his decision-making. This is another example of how deeply virtual reality penetrated actual political reality.

While everyone else was jockeying for attention, the president was trying to get through his agenda. Zelenskyy favored fact-based decision-making, which he hoped would have a direct, positive effect on the lives of real people. Raised in a provincial city himself, he was very familiar with how ordinary people in the regions lived. And as a businessman, he also clearly understood the challenges of running a business in the years after Ukraine proclaimed its independence. But he really wanted to change things.

On my trips with the president and in Kyiv itself, I met many businessmen who thanked the staff for Zelenskyy's decisions: they were able to get credit for business loans in the tens of billions of hryvnias with an interest rate in the range of 5, 7, or 9 percent—this was very generous support for businesses in the country, where the interest rate charged on credit used to be as high as 20 percent. The new government was intent on fostering private investment and helping businesses take part in large projects in partnership with the state.

In addition, the new government introduced more favorable market conditions in the agricultural sector thanks to the long-awaited and historic land reform legislation. The multipronged program, which was finally implemented in 2020, lifted a two-decade-long moratorium on the sale of arable land. Although the moratorium had served large companies very well, smaller farmers had been unable to use their land as collateral for further investment and improvement. Many were unable to properly care for their land. This new reform legislation included World Bank–funded subsidies for farmers and strategies for government investment and irrigation and drainage that would be implemented over the next decade. It would also help make Ukraine's agricultural sector, its biggest export industry, more transparent and productive. Ukraine is famous for having 25 to 30 percent of the world's most fertile black soil, and 70 percent of its land is agricultural. This reform package was long overdue and promised to have a large impact on future GDP numbers.

"We see what you are doing for business. We see how your team is working. Thank you, really," an entrepreneurs remarked, even though we were unable to help him with guarantees from the Deposit Guarantee Fund.

Zelenskyy always repeated that entrepreneurship builds on its own efforts, helping to improve the country's economy, and government should not interfere, control, or get in the way. On the contrary, the government should create conditions for it to develop.

This is why the discussions and decisions about COVID-19 lockdowns were carefully debated among the ministers. The first lockdown had been enacted in late March and lasted for two months, and as in every country, it had financial and political repercussions, but it was instrumental in staving off the first wave of the virus. After cases began to rise in the final months of 2020, several government representatives advocated introducing a second strict lockdown in early December. But the president disagreed. Everyone needed to do their year-end financial accounting, and the economy needed a boost from the big year-end retail sales. So the second lockdown was delayed until January 2021. That was a time when people would find it more convenient to stay at home, with all kinds of special New Year's dishes to eat and frost fastening its grip outside.

It is difficult to build a state when you are starting not from scratch, but from something that has already been thoroughly worn out, ripped off, and smashed up. It is no easy task. Even when I was working two jobs before I joined Zelenskyy's government, I was never as tired as when I was serving as the president's press secretary. Our staff was not even close to being as large as that of the preceding heads of state. Prior to the rise of social media, the communications departments comprised around fifty to sixty members. During my tenure, there were only about forty of us, operating in a much more difficult and information-rich environment than had previously existed.

Other departments also had problems with staff recruitment, turnover, and budgets. The majority, however, worked unsparingly, knowing they had received their best opportunity in politics, thanks to their boss, and that it would be very easy to lose it. By the second year of his presidency, Zelenskyy began to give his team a chance for career advancement. Some parliamentarians were appointed to ministerial posts, a team of spokespersons was formed, and a "one voice" policy, a practice drawn from management consulting, was instituted across the entire government. The new faces began to look more like real politicians. Zelenskyy worked hard to assemble his team, clean it up, and then nurture it as a political force. This was his businesslike approach in Ukrainian politics, and it appeared to be working.

CHAPTER 5

Seeking Peace in Donbas

But in today's world, where we live, there is no
longer someone else's war. None of you can feel safe
when there is a war in Ukraine, when there is a war
in Europe.

—VOLODYMYR ZELENSKYY

TO THE UN GENERAL ASSEMBLY, SEPTEMBER 25, 2019

Whenever we see the Ukrainian president on television, our view is very limited—a short speech in a video provided by the press service. Only the president's team knows how hard it is to prepare for these appearances: scheduling flights and transfers to multiple regions in one trip; communicating with the military on trips to "zero" positions, as the frontline positions are called; preparing reports and speeches; resolving off-road lack of connection; setting up live broadcasts; providing accommodations, food, water, toilets, gas . . . the list goes on forever.

No one knows, for instance, that on this trip to Donbas during the 2020 cease-fire, a young woman in a nearby helicopter is carefully tending the flowers destined for the memorial so that they do not get windblown, so that a journalist who leans over to look out a window does not crush them; no one knows how she carefully unpacks them so the protocol service can present the flowers to the president at the proper moment.

No one notices a soldier in uniform who vigilantly guards us, looking out of the helicopter, leaning toward his machine gun as he diligently performs his duty. A Reuters photographer sits opposite him, snapping one photo after another.

A Reuters journalist, eager for details, carefully records her impressions. She is very nervous. This is her first such assignment. Her flimsy sandals with heels reveal this.

I answer her questions and advise her to drink less, because there will be almost no toilets, and not to read a lot and not to look out the window, because she might throw up on this, her first flight on a helicopter, and not to use cellular communications, because the Russians will intercept them.

Everyone who flies on these trips for the first time always snaps landscapes from the window, beautiful Ukrainian landscapes: fields, lakes, rivers, dense forests. There are almost no roads in Donbas.

The waiter, dressed in camouflage, who has been on such flights before, no longer takes any pictures. He is experienced enough now to be able to master his fear and focus on his job, which requires organization and resourcefulness. Nothing surprises him now.

At the end of the flight, the young woman brings the flowers to the protocol officer. The young woman, the officer, and the waiter struggle to close the round window of the helicopter so that the wind does not damage the bouquets. The president and his team will place them at the new monument to those who died during the war in Donbas.

The president often goes off script when he speaks to the soldiers. On this trip, one of many, they are being awarded medals. He speaks directly to them without microphones; almost nothing he says is audible to the assembled press: "It is a great honor for me to be here at the dedication of such a monument. Our simple, heroic Ukrainian words are inscribed on it: 'We are fighting for something priceless, for the Motherland. We have only one Motherland. We have only one—Ukraine. And we can't lose it. And we will never lose. On the contrary, we will return everything to Ukraine.'

"Now, during the last ten days, we have suffered no wounded, no dead. First of all, I am grateful to you that you protect your comrades. And this is important. It is important that a full and comprehensive cease-fire be implemented in the war zone in Donbas. . . . It is important that whenever we hear that someone wants to attack us, even a minor attack, you will always respond effectively."

The president bestows awards on the masked soldiers, then approaches the press to answer a few questions about Donbas and the peace initiative. The local journalists are different from colleagues elsewhere. Here they don't hype or fool around. They clearly know the value of words and the value of information. People learn from war in different ways.

We make additional visits to frontline positions. On the way to the parking lot afterward, the car breaks down. Most of the other cars were delayed. Anything can happen, and everything can be dealt with, one way or another. We drive some more.

Then a few more awards are given out while we wait. Several people accompany the president to check on the frontline positions. I send Reuters with them.

There will be three more stops in other cities, at different positions along the line. The president engages with the soldiers, listens to what they say about the cease-fire. For many soldiers, this is an unexpected turn of events, but each of them wants peace in Donbas. Over the past ten days, no one has died or been wounded from shelling, but several soldiers have died from health problems. Every morning the president receives these statistics.

In Bakhmut, about fifty-five miles from Donetsk, the administrative center of one of the two Donbas regions, Zelenskyy decides to go to the grocery store. The whole delegation stops and goes inside the shop for coffee and sweets. We run after him and take a few photos. People are happy to see Zelenskyy: they ask for a selfie, call friends and relatives to brag about having seen the president. Some online critics will suspect that this was a deliberate PR stunt. They are wrong: it was definitely not deliberate.

We sleep in the local hospital. For me, it's like a childhood memory. The daughter of a neonatologist and a pathologist, I often hung around the mortuary museum and spent the night in the neonatal ward, waiting for my parents. In this Donbas hospital, I ask not to be accommodated in the gynecological department.

We are assigned bunks in the wards and nursing quarters. Some of the wards have showers, and there are several toilets in the one-story building. My backpack disappears. I decide to share a room with the young florist, who had the good luck to get a room with all the amenities. Fortunately, my backpack is found and returned within an hour.

———

During those years, Zelenskyy made frequent trips to Donbas: eighteen in 2019–2020. He spent every military holiday in Donbas. Once, we drove over sixty miles along the demarcation line. Another time he walked with the president of Switzerland to the bridge where, on the other side, Russian-backed separatist militants stood guard, armed with machine guns.

For Zelenskyy, the issue of peace was personal. In less than a year as president, he managed to secure the return of some 150 prisoners of war from Russia, Crimea, and Donbas. He also revived the Normandy Format peace talks, during which the leaders of Ukraine, Germany, France, and Russia agreed on a path to peace.

Zelenskyy's rise to power had improved the prospects for peace in Donbas. The Kremlin had long since ended its dialogue with Poroshenko, leaving no chance to achieve peace. The dialogue between two warring countries could not have been resumed with just any Ukrainian politician. It was unlikely that Putin would have talked with a hypernationalist Ukrainian president. Moreover, it was also highly improbable that even an experienced Ukrainian politician from the old guard would have been able to maintain a dialogue for as long as Zelenskyy did.

Unfortunately, it turned out that Ukraine was threatened by an internal enemy as well. After being in power from 2014 to 2019, Poroshenko did not really accept his defeat at the polls, even after the electorate overwhelmingly rejected his bid for a second term. Instead, he tried to undermine his successor at every turn. His supporters continued to push the false narrative that Zelenskyy was supposedly pro-Russian, the strongest negative image they could think to put out there in 2019 in Ukraine.

For five years, Ukraine under Poroshenko had existed in a state of somnambulism vis-à-vis Russia. The pointless, hypocritical stories about a new Ukrainian identity invented by Poroshenko supporters created the illusion that they were patriotic. Sadly, however, there was nothing inventive in their formula; they dredged up hackneyed idols from Ukrainian history and failed to say anything new or meaningful about how we might move forward as a country.

Poroshenko's love for the Ukrainian language was as hypocritical as his patriotism. He considered Russian-speaking Ukrainians unpatriotic and enacted a law just after he lost the 2019 election declaring that all civil servants, soldiers, doctors, and teachers must speak Ukrainian, which antagonized Russian speakers and was a particularly sensitive issue in the Russian-speaking areas of the country near Donbas. All the while, he cynically ignored the fact that his own family's native language is Russian. He put on an embroidered shirt and arranged magnificent parades with military equipment, even while the "Ilovaisk cauldron"—in which a botched withdrawal of trapped Ukrainian soldiers led to a massacre perpetrated by Russian troops that took at least four hundred lives—was taking place in Donbas. It was one of the most terrible massacres in this country, until now.

Poroshenko pompously opposed Russia in his speeches and then promoted more and more news from Russia on Ukrainian TV channels—news that was derogatory, accusatory, snide, and disgustingly low-grade. He placed all responsibility for the war in Donbas on Putin, but at the same time, he became friends with Putin's crony and representative in Ukraine, Viktor Medvedchuk. (Medvedchuk, the "dark prince" of Ukrainian politics, had long promoted Putin's interests in Ukraine, undermining the state by pushing pro-Russian narratives and policies.) Paradoxically, while purporting to distance himself from Russia, Poroshenko did everything possible to adopt its mindset. For the five long years of his administration, Ukraine seemed to be staring into a Russian looking glass.

Ukraine was simply unprepared, too, for the Russian propaganda, a powerful Kremlin weapon used to bludgeon our country after the invasion of Donbas and that continues even now. By deciding to introduce Russian methods of manipulation, fake news, and counterpropaganda into Ukraine to counteract Russian disinformation, Poroshenko and his government partially discredited themselves as a reliable partner in the eyes of the world. In 2015, foreign journalists who had come to Ukraine to cover the Revolution of Dignity and the war in Donbas warned both the Ukrainian authorities and the media about these tactics. Russian news had long since become entirely untrustworthy, they said, by hiding the truth and spreading lies, while Ukraine still had a chance to establish its reputation as an honest partner.

In any case, Ukraine could not afford to invest anything like the amount of resources that Moscow invests in propaganda. And, of course, we did not have a network of overseas propaganda parrots like Russia Today.

Zelenskyy's administration took some immediate steps to fight disinformation but never followed through with additional measures. But even so, by 2022, Ukraine was better prepared

than it had been. In the eight years since the first Russian invasion in 2014, Ukrainian journalists had developed many successful independent media projects that reached millions. They
verified information as well as they could and cooperated with
the military authorities to spread reliable information carefully
and quickly. They were trying to find a healthy balance between
the need to raise morale among the population and provide ver-
ifiable facts. Ukraine also developed a responsible civil society
that was helpful in many ways, as volunteers on the front lines
and as news commentators for foreign media. All this created a
chorus of Ukrainian voices in the information war with Russia.
In this way, Ukraine has become very effective in showing the
truth to the world.

The war of 2022 also put on hold previous intense internal
disagreements about the ways to achieve peace—first, because
the existing peace agreements were now null and void, and
second, because the authorities were forced to band together
in order to face an external aggressor that was determined to
destroy our country.

After the first invasion of Donbas, treaties called the Minsk
Agreements were formulated. They included impossible conditions for Ukraine. One of the most unacceptable was that Russia
required that elections to determine the fate of the occupied
territory would be held before their troops withdrew. This of
course meant that the election would be conducted by the oc-
cupiers, and there would be a 99.9 percent probability that the
territory would be transferred to the Kremlin-supported armed
separatists. As Zelenskyy emphatically said many times, this
meant holding elections at gunpoint, in the absence of interna-

tional observers, without democratic procedures in place and without transparency. Under such conditions, Ukraine would be unable to control those districts of Donbas where hostilities were continuing, territories controlled by the armed separatists who would monopolize the local councils. This was the key issue that Zelenskyy clearly identified, saying that the sequence must be: first, Ukrainian government control, and only then, elections.

Once, in a telephone conversation, French president Emmanuel Macron emphasized the common ground that united him with Zelenskyy in these negotiations: neither of them had signed these earlier agreements, but both had no viable option other than to build on these unsatisfactory accords as a basis for achieving peace.

The Ukrainian authorities were unable to find common ground on the Minsk Agreements with Russia. But there was another alternative: earlier, there had been something called the Normandy Format, talks that had existed in parallel to the Minsk Agreements. The four countries that took part—Ukraine, Russia, Germany, and France—first met in Normandy to try to resolve the situation in Donbas in 2014. The talks broke down in 2016 and had not been reconvened since then, as Putin refused to meet. During those three years of continued hostilities, we were grimly compiling statistics about the destruction from Russian shelling and noting the numbers of wounded and killed every day. Zelenskyy managed to reconvene this group, and the leaders from the four nations met in Paris on December 9, 2019, to resume the dialogue for peace.

We arrived for the meeting in Paris buoyed by support in the international arena. The United States and Great Britain were firmly supporting Ukraine, and Zelenskyy had already managed to establish warm relations with Germany and France. Having the most powerful woman in the world, Angela Merkel, on our side was important. But also winning the support of Macron meant that the ratio at the negotiating table was three to one.

To her great credit, First Lady Olena Zelenska played an important role in our relations with France. She had managed to hit it off with Brigitte Macron during her first visit to Paris in June 2019. Because of this, a warm relationship developed between the first couples of Ukraine and France. And over time, it grew even stronger.

Few people get the privilege of walking along the hidden corridors inside the Élysée Palace. One feels the weight of so many historical events that took place in that three-hundred-year-old building. Many famous figures have met there and made decisions that changed the course of history. The institutional memory of France is stored not only in the grandiose, red-carpeted reception rooms, replete with floral paintings, marble, and gilt trim. It also can be found in the more modest rooms of fifteen to twenty square meters that have been cleverly converted into modern meeting rooms, discreetly hidden in the nooks and crannies of corridors behind inconspicuous doors. How many plans of war and peace have these walls seen? Here the first French emperor, Napoléon Bonaparte, lived, and here he abdicated.

Macron's political ambition was to become the leader of the new Europe, and, as a result, he wanted to lead the effort to end the only ongoing war in Europe. Even though that war was being fought outside the boundaries of the European Union, it was Ukrainian territory, and Ukraine is in Europe.

In 2021, after the German elections, Chancellor Merkel handed over her post to her successor. The European Union watched from afar, but not without interest, as the new head of one of the most powerful countries came to power, and wondered how Germany's domestic and foreign policy would change, how Germany's relations with Russia and Brussels would develop, and whether the Nord Stream 2 natural gas pipeline between Russia and Germany would be completed. Although it was not apparent then, Germany's decision to rely on Russia for its energy needs and its underestimation of Russia's threat to Ukraine—and to the EU—would put it in a difficult position when the EU adopted sanctions against Russia in 2022.

This leadership succession, which had not occurred in a long time—Merkel had been chancellor for sixteen years—inevitably weakened German influence as the new chancellor found his footing and provided France with a strong competitive opportunity. The ongoing war in Ukraine added urgency. Those who ended it, bringing peace to the long-suffering Ukrainians, could expect laurels, perhaps even the Nobel Peace Prize.

Zelenskyy did everything possible as president to secure support for Ukraine in the international arena. Under his presidency, relations between Ukraine and France reached a level that had never been seen before. Nevertheless, in an interview with the well-known French publication *Le Figaro* before a trip to Paris in April 2021, Zelenskyy boldly described both his relationship with Macron and what, in his opinion, France could do for Ukraine:

> *It seems to me that President Macron wants to be on friendly terms with Russia—I understand him. But he must understand my desire, which I spoke of. It always hurts less if it doesn't concern you, and it always seems like it won't happen to you. But*

*history doesn't pat you on the head, it hits you when you don't
expect it to. You have to be ready. What is it like to be ready? To
have such countries, such friends, such presidents who have your
back, so you do not need to be afraid.*

Zelenskyy viewed the Ukrainian people themselves as the most important ally in achieving peace. The desire to end the war topped
all the polls. At that time, around fourteen thousand people had
already died in Donbas. It was the most heavily mined territory in
the world, once home to millions who abandoned it on the run. It
was a land of suffering, poverty, fear, and pain.

Russia, of course, depicted the military conflict in Donbas as
internal strife caused by radical nationalist movements in Ukraine,
a claim that some politicians tried to support with pictures on TV.
But there has never been homegrown separatism in Ukraine. As
Oleksiy Reznikov, then minister for reintegration of the temporarily occupied territories (a position created under Zelenskyy) and
later the defense minister of Ukraine, said, we have a "smuggling
of ideologies" from neighboring Russia, which it injects into the
hearts and minds of people through propaganda as part of a hybrid war of conventional, irregular, and cyber warfare with other
types of influence, from fake news and rigged elections to diplomacy. "Responses in a hybrid war should be only hybrid," Reznikov
said. Before Zelenskyy's administration, Ukraine had already tried
to reestablish control of these territories by uttering proud, war-
like cries while parading with torches in hand. This formula did
not work to bring about the return of Donbas. Now Zelenskyy had
launched another method: soft power. This approach was much
more complicated—more "hybrid," if you like—but it yielded results. It also included a fight against disinformation, both external

and internal, and help for the inhabitants of the region through social assistance and job creation to rebuild the region. All these efforts contributed toward creating an attractive image of Ukraine that accorded with reality.

Everyone had expected that in 2014 or 2015 France and Germany would come to an agreement with Russia and that the Kremlin would withdraw its troops from Donbas. But diplomacy did not work, and their efforts came to naught. I remembered the famous saying attributed to Bismarck: "The agreements signed by Russia aren't worth the price of the sheet of paper they are written on."

The expectations in 2019 arising from the renewed Normandy Format, with Zelenskyy instead of Poroshenko and Macron instead of the previous French leader, François Hollande, were enormous. The media scrupulously sought out the details of the meeting. For a whole week new information was presented every day. However, we tried to prepare people for these high expectations to end in disappointment. We immediately explained that the war in Donbas would not be resolved the next day and that we must be ready for that eventuality.

At home, various political actors within Ukraine continued to undermine all attempts to achieve peace in order to increase their standing in the polls. One could argue that it was good politics, but it was certainly not an example of real leadership, nor was it in the interests of the Ukrainian people. Some demonstrators called the prospect of peace talks "surrender," but we in the communications office reminded them that the peace initiative involved a list of concrete actions to be achieved, not surrender. The first was to properly restore a bridge destroyed by the war in Stanytsia Luhanska in Luhansk Oblast, one of the contested areas of Ukraine. This bridge was very important, because every day thousands of people crossed the line of demarcation by means of it. The bridge linked Russian separatist–held territory to Ukrainian territory. People of all ages dragged their luggage across a tall, hastily constructed pedestrian bridge with steep stairs at either end, ascending and descending the treacherous walkway in all kinds of weather: snow, rain, slush. When Zelenskyy first visited Stanytsia Luhanska, the local people asked for two things: that he build a new bridge for them and pay their pensions. On November 20, after much skepticism from his opponents, Zelenskyy opened the bridge two days earlier than the planned date.

There were also quite a lot of cries of "betrayal" because of false reports that our troops had pulled back at three points along the front lines. But afterward, there really was a withdrawal on both sides. The fortifications were removed and the territory cleared of mines. There was no shelling, and no one died. For the first time in years, local residents felt what life was like without war.

In an interview with the foreign publications *Time*, *Le Monde*, *Der Spiegel*, and *Gazeta Wyborcza* a week before the Normandy Format peace talks, Zelenskyy said that he would not go to war over Donbas. Aggression could only breed more aggression, he explained. In the event of an attempt to achieve peace by military means, we would lose hundreds of thousands of lives and provoke an economic crisis. There would be more orphans, more wounded, and more displaced persons. And even with all that pain, our victory could not be guaranteed. This fact was always overlooked by those who called for peace through war.

The Ukrainian army gets its strength from its determination to fight for our land, our people, our future. But the ability to fight is not the measure of real strength. The truly strong are those who can prevent the endless deaths and horrors of war. So, instead of fighting in 2019, Ukraine chose to have a dialogue with the enemy. We did our best to behave like a civilized country. We looked for a way out through diplomacy.

"Politics is not an exact science," Zelenskyy said in his interview. "That's why in school I loved mathematics. Everything in mathematics was clear to me. You can solve an equation with a variable, with one variable. But here it's only variables, including the politicians in our country. I don't know these people. I can't understand what dough they're made of. That's why I think nobody can have any trust. Everybody just has their interests." He went to Paris to defend the interests of Ukraine.

It was a warm winter day in December 2019. Hundreds of journalists from Russia and many European countries stood in line for the opportunity to attend a press conference following the negotiations with the leaders of the "Normandy Four." I remember well how the press service of the Élysée Palace was flustered by such a huge number of reporters, especially from Ukraine—more than seventy journalists. I remember how its staffers lost their lists and we helped find them.

We were the first to enter the hall where the negotiations were to take place, followed by the Russian delegation. I had the immediate impression that the Russians were a bit tentative about introducing themselves. The setup for the conference was not yet complete, so I went to ask someone for the Wi-Fi password while we waited. The manager didn't know it, but he tried to help me find it. One of the members of the Russian delegation followed us, because he also needed the password. When he approached us, he didn't speak to the Frenchman but instead addressed me in French. I could see the Cyrillic writing on his name tag, so I replied in Russian that I didn't speak French. That really surprised him. "You speak Russian?" he asked. "Yes, Russian," I replied.

This proved to him that the Russian narrative that Ukrainian "nationalists" were opposed to speaking Russian was false. That made me feel good. It was a little thing that only the two of us could understand. As soon as I answered him, the Frenchman found the password for the Wi-Fi, but I had made my point.

I remember everything to the smallest detail as if it were yesterday, especially the feeling of being close to those who would decide the fate of my country according to how the negotiations went. I remember the nervous tension when the leaders sat down at the round table. With bated breath, we hung on every emotion, every movement, as half the world watched along with us.

Each delegation and its leader had their own goals and position, but they were united in one thing: all of them listened intently to President Zelenskyy every time he spoke.

He spoke from the heart, expressing pain for his country, where Ukrainian citizens were dying almost every day in the war in the eastern region of Donbas. All the delegations were surprised by Zelenskyy's very concrete negotiating positions. He wouldn't let them off the hook. As soon as he realized that they were trying to shelve some important issue for Ukraine, he took the floor and said, "Let's do it again." Somehow, by this method, he convinced the others that he was right and that the issue they were discussing still belonged on the diplomatic agenda, and so protected his country's interests. Thanks to his adroit diplomacy, three statements in the final communiqué were changed in favor of Ukraine. This was not just Zelenskyy's success but also Ukraine's.

I am often asked about my impressions of Putin, because few people have ever seen him in person as I have. I always reply that there is only one way to describe Putin: "old age." No matter how much I looked at him and his delegation, no matter how much I listened, everything about them conveyed old age: old ideology, old principles, old behavior, old thoughts. His entire team seemed hopelessly outdated. And when I found the right words to describe how I saw him, I suddenly became calmer. The universe cannot allow old age to dominate forever. The world around us is constantly changing; even five years represents an abyss between generations. Old age cannot survive that much change.

During the negotiations, Putin kept his head down most of the time. He clearly felt uncomfortable. Every now and then he called someone over from his team to verify some point of information. Sometimes he avoided giving direct answers to questions, saying that he didn't have the facts and they must be checked. He kept repeating himself, stammering, and pausing, spitting out that Russia was not a participant in the military conflict in Donbas, although everyone at the table knew that was not true.

At the end of the conference, before the communiqués were finalized, Zelenskyy was chatting with Chancellor Merkel and President Macron. Putin, on the other hand, was standing on his own in another room with his press secretary. He chose not to join his counterparts, preferring to withdraw from them, as if he didn't agree with anything that was happening. Then he disappeared for a few minutes, delaying the end of the conference.

In thinking about it later, it was a rather ridiculous moment: one of the most aggressive and ruthless dictators, who inspired fear in so many people, walked out of the room, past the press, and down the hall with his head down and an enigmatic half-smile on his face. Immediately, journalists from all over the world rushed over to take pictures or videos of him as he left.

One journalist turned to me and asked excitedly, "Where is he going?" And I replied, "To wash his hands."

Putin did not expect that a leader who had been president for only a few months at the time of the meeting would be so fully informed and would sit directly opposite him, and that his vote would outweigh Putin's. Zelenskyy spoke pragmatically about concrete, workable approaches, rejecting all the old assumptions that had been in place since the Minsk Agreements.

For a very long time, Putin had been refining his image as a KGB thug, and then as a dictator and a monster capable of the horrors of mass murder and war. Few people, however, thought about one important aspect of this leader's psychology: Putin knew how to give orders, but he didn't know how to negotiate. That was why the negotiations in the Normandy Format were difficult for him. And he never agreed to meet again.

In 2022, he ignored Zelenskyy's invitation to negotiate. For more than two decades, no one had contradicted him, nor had anyone been willing to bring him bad news. This made Putin a weak negotiator. Instead, he used only blackmail and various instruments of war to negotiate.

Zelenskyy, on the other hand, could not be more different. He is a master negotiator, and he has done everything he can to bring about peace in Ukraine and security for his people. Peace means everything to him. Only with peace can he focus on rebuilding his nation.

———

A tiny shop in a village not far from Marinka in Donbas was never empty. A mere forty-three square feet in size, it used to sell ice cream, canned food, vegetables, fruit, and alcohol. And somewhat unusually for a store like this, there was air-conditioning.

The shopkeeper, a young brunette, said that after a bomb hit the roof, they had to make minor repairs. But they were going to move out soon in order to make more extensive renovations.

"And what will Zelenskyy be doing?" she asked me when I came in to buy an ice cream.

I said that the president was traveling around Donbas for two days, visiting the front lines and speaking with the troops.

"If only this would bring peace," said the young woman.

The word we had heard most often from civilians and military in Donbas before the large-scale invasion in 2022 was "peace." Wherever you looked, whomever you asked, everyone was tired of living close to war, which brought sadness, pain, and poverty. It was the duty of every politician, everyone who cared about Ukraine, to do everything possible to return people, territories, and peace to our land. Exactly twenty days after this conversation, on July 27, 2020, a new agreement on a comprehensive and extensive cease-fire came into effect in Donbas. This was the longest and most disputed cease-fire in the six and a half years of the war. In any military conflict, "cease-fire" and "truce" are fragile rather than stable concepts. It was difficult to imagine that a territory crammed with weapons and explosives, where Russian-backed separatist mercenaries were fighting, would fall silent all at once. The demarcation line extended for more than 250 miles. There, from each side of it, contradictory worldviews, fears, anger, impotence, poverty, and dashed hopes converged.

On our side of the demarcation line, the headquarters of the Joint Forces Operation never tired of repeating every second that they were ready for real military operations, to protect territory and people. No one would accuse the Ukrainian army of cowardice. Strength and resilience were what characterized our warriors.

And yet, however unstable this cease-fire, we lived weeks and months during which the war did not claim a single one of our soldiers. . . .

According to the Organization for Security and Co-operation in Europe, more than eighteen thousand violations were recorded in the five weeks before the cease-fire began and more than a thousand in the seven weeks after. At the end of the year, there were forty-nine combat casualties in the Joint Forces Operation zone: forty-five people who died before the start of the truce and only four after. About twenty were wounded. According to the General Staff, during the same period in 2019, thirty-six people were killed and 129 injured. In 2018, fifty-one were killed and 304 were injured. In 2017, sixty were killed and 308 were wounded. These figures speak of one thing: no matter what provocations occurred, the cease-fire agreements had borne some fruit. And even if the situation was far from perfect, a shopkeeper from a village near Marinka in 2020 had already begun to remember what it was like to hear silence. Like her, we all hoped that peace would soon come to Donbas.

But now our entire country has been invaded, and Marinka has been destroyed.

CHAPTER 6

The Press vs. the President

Acquiring power is difficult, but it is even harder to maintain it. In the case of Ukraine, rife with naysayers and weak, still-developing institutions, it was often difficult to keep the machinery of government on track as Zelenskyy moved forcefully ahead.

Making things even more difficult was the behavior of defeated ex-president Petro Poroshenko. He had not come to terms with his crushing defeat at the polls and refused to grant Zelenskyy the authority that comes with a smooth democratic transition of power. Instead of retreating quietly from political life as former U.S. presidents typically do, he continued to play president, making frequent policy pronouncements to the press, holding meetings with foreign leaders when he traveled abroad, staging political rallies and protests, and, in effect, doing everything he could to create a parallel political universe, stoking division in an already raw and fractured country. He went so far as to deliver an address on one of his TV channels on New Year's Eve, scheduling it just before Zelenskyy's own address, the customary one usually given by the nation's president.

Despite Poroshenko's poor conduct, Zelenskyy remained undaunted. During his run for the presidency, Zelenskyy had won over the public with the help of his sharp wit and charm. He established himself as a fighter of corruption by exposing the outgoing oligarch Poroshenko's misdeeds—for example, Zelenskyy drew attention to his opponent's cronyism and the government contracts he awarded to his friends. Zelenskyy's four-month campaign succeeded in getting control of that narrative. He forced a far more experienced opponent to respond to his straightforward talk and clever pokes. A political novice, he was, nonetheless, entirely unafraid. He showed the people of Ukraine that they had been exploited by their leadership.

For his first eight months or so in office, President Zelenskyy enjoyed the usual postelection honeymoon. He basked in his constituents' love. Everything negative could be explained as the work of his predecessor, now cast aside. Only positive developments lay ahead. It can even be said that this period led Zelenskyy to fall into the easiest trap for a novice politician: flushed with the overconfidence of victory, he developed blind spots, momentarily forgetting that any democratically elected leader can be defeated later. As most people know, the battle for hearts and minds does not end after winning an election, passing a law, or even succeeding on a battlefield. And governing a fractious country of forty million never ends.

Zelenskyy began his presidency with much of the same team in place that had been with him throughout the campaign. Unsurprisingly, his early agenda-setting employed much of the same rhetoric, methods, and conduct that had swept him to his brilliant victory. The administration felt comfortable with the same playbook that won the election, and it worked to an extent, but the long-term weaknesses of certain practices and the lack or limitations of critical personnel began to emerge as the responsibilities of office became more apparent. It was the old political story that the team that got you elected may not be the best team to govern the country.

During the presidential campaign, Zelenskyy almost never gave interviews. His managers, including Kyrylo Tymoshenko, who became a deputy chief of staff in his office and was responsible for communications, believed there was no need for a presidential candidate to allow the media to mediate between him and the public. The theory was that political messaging could—and should—come directly, thereby fully controlled by Zelenskyy himself. Andriy Bohdan, Zelenskyy's first chief of staff, made this clear when he was quoted saying as much to Radio Free Europe: "We interact with society without intermediaries and without journalists." The offhand statement by an official member of Zelenskyy's team served as a declaration that journalists would not be respected or considered crucial to the maintenance of democratic order in Zelenskyy's Ukraine.

Those words created a huge brouhaha that damaged the president, his press office, and me, as press secretary. There are some statements that are just impossible to walk back or soften, and this was one of them—especially so because at the time there was more than a measure of truth to Bohdan's statement. We had allowed ourselves to become insular and detached from the public's voice. We were prohibited from responding to media inquiries and were forced to refuse all interviews, regardless of whether they came from some unknown outlet or a credible worldwide news organization like CNN. The ham-handed treatment of the media became particularly intense when, at the beginning of August 2019, a fake resignation letter from the president's chief of staff began to circulate on social media accounts. According to the letter, addressed to the president, the chief of staff supposedly asked to be dismissed. But the chief of staff's deputy—who some accused of circulating the letter himself—prohibited the press office from publicly correcting the record on the matter. We had to turn off our phones at the very moment we should have made a disclaimer to clear the air. We were not allowed to either confirm or deny the letter's veracity. As it turned out, Chief of Staff Bohdan was indeed dismissed several months later, in February 2020, but the rules for dealing with the media still remained in place for some time and continued to cause problems.

Worst of all, the information vacuum created by our silence was quickly filled by criticism from Zelenskyy's most ruthless opponents. Everyone was listening to Petro Poroshenko, the media mogul and politician, and disgraced Ukrainian oligarch Ihor Kolomoyskyy. They were among the antidemocratic actors who used their own media outlets to extend their influence. No one was listening to us. No matter how many times we insisted that journalists were essential in building a modern democratic society, and even after Bohdan's exit, the relationship between the media and the President's Office remained testy. The problems even extended to the international press. In retrospect, this seems ironic, considering how positively Zelenskyy is viewed now as the leader of the Ukrainian resistance.

When I started as press secretary in June 2019, I took it upon myself to improve relations with the media, seeing how much

Zelenskyy's message had been hampered by his team's outdated approach. I was severely reproached by my superiors for agreeing to interviews with German and French publications, despite the fact that Zelenskyy himself approved them and was pleased with their outcomes. Even the president's critics at the time praised messages we had sent to Germany's Chancellor Merkel and France's President Macron on his behalf. Still, a core group of entrenched power players within the administration was furious at me. I received a tongue-lashing for leaking information, and members of the Office of the President were told not to speak to me. I was not included on the next trip abroad, to Canada, and an interview between President Zelenskyy and a leading Canadian publication, the *Globe and Mail*, was canceled.

Despite the setbacks, I continued to push my views internally. I believed strongly that the team's unwillingness to let Zelenskyy speak to the press sent the wrong message to the public and had begun to reflect poorly on the president himself. The Ukrainian diaspora in Canada, a powerful group of loyal supporters of our country, had eagerly awaited the opportunity to hear from the promising new Ukrainian head of state. Instead, his overly controlled visit had almost become an insult to that community. And back home in Ukraine, Poroshenko took advantage of the misstep. He worked the local press to generate the impression that the Ukrainian diaspora should be suspicious of Zelenskyy's pro-Russia leanings, artfully concealed by Zelenskyy's impenetrable team. Still, the president and the press office remained silent. Undaunted, I continued my campaign, scoring one small press hit, an interview on Deutsche Welle, the state-owned German broadcaster.

Of course, infighting inside political organizations is not

necessarily unusual. But the relationship between President Zelenskyy, his Office of the President, and the supporting teams assembled to build the new Ukraine that we had all envisioned began to resemble the palace intrigues one might see on a Netflix series, not an administration nurturing a young democracy. My rookie standing on Zelenskyy's team made it difficult to confront the successful and wealthy men who had helped elect him and now sought to exert their influence on his policies in office. And even his more experienced Kvartal 95 colleagues in the press office—people who had already worked with Zelenskyy for upward of ten years—struggled to make headway. Our explanation that this problem was not in the press office or the media, but more a clash of outlooks, fell on deaf ears. The higher-ups were businessmen who didn't understand that a president whose popularity hinged on his rejection of the old political system must be accessible and accountable. And in a democracy, that accountability comes from the press. Transparency is everything. Only after Zelenskyy's approval ratings began to suffer (in January 2020 it was 59 percent of support compared with a record 73 percent in April 2019) did we see any real progress toward thawing relations with the press.

Soon, Zelenskyy better appreciated the need for a relationship with the press and took a more strategic approach to communication. Press conferences became more frequent; during these sessions, he not only spoke but took questions from the assembled journalists. We also started providing responses to media requests, and interviews with international and Ukrainian journalists became a part of our routine. Those opinions, like mine, that had supported a more free-flowing communication with the public had started to win out.

The notion that remaining strong and silent is the only route to effective leadership has become outdated since the advent of online media. The world is noisier than ever, public figures outside politics are ever present on social media, and wealthy individuals have a newfound ability to broadcast their values to mass audiences at will. To be silent in that environment is to be absent. As we saw in Ukraine, the onslaught of third-party actors attempting to influence public opinion required a multidimensional response from the government.

The one place, however, where silence really was the best option was in the delicate diplomatic negotiations involving people's lives. I saw this in action as the Ukrainian government worked through back-channel negotiations to secure a prisoner exchange with Russia for thirty-five Ukrainians: eleven activists, some of them captured for disagreeing with Russia's illegal annexation of Crimea in 2014 (including the film director Oleg Sentsov, whose 2021 film *Rhino*, the story of an aggressive delinquent who works his way up the criminal hierarchy in 1990s Ukraine, had its premiere at the Venice Film Festival), and twenty-four sailors seized in a November 2018 Russian attack and given a harsh sentence in a remote Russian prison in the far north of the country. As negotiations progressed for their release, and despite attacks launched against us in the interim, Ukraine's diplomatic professionals maintained total secrecy. In a politically charged negotiation such as this one, that secrecy was necessary to ensure that negotiations could continue without undue interference.

But that almost didn't happen. In June 2019, Zelenskyy held an off-the-record meeting with journalists to explain his decisions regarding the prisoner exchange talks. He requested that the reporters write nothing for two weeks while he sought the return of the prisoners, but negotiations with Russia were always protracted. After two weeks, some internet reporters began to post angry messages, saying they had done everything asked of them to observe the media blackout, but that time had run out and they could no longer remain silent.

In my view, these reporters' behavior demonstrated not only a misunderstanding of diplomatic procedure but also a lack of ethics and appreciation for the efforts we all had made internally to share the president's thinking on the matter. Why choose this time, one of immense sensitivity in regard to human life and Ukraine's relationship with Russia, to disrupt that positive trend? Sentsov and some of his compatriots had languished in Russian prisons for five years. The possibility of bringing back these men was so fragile, yet so ardently desired, that it seemed people, including journalists, simply could not control their emotions. Every week, the Russians raised some other issue that made the return of the men seem more elusive: they haggled over which Ukrainians they would release and for whom, how Ukraine would comment on different geopolitical matters, and whether the new leadership was ready for dialogue and compromise. Russia is a very difficult negotiating partner. For the most part, it manipulates and pressures, demands and blackmails. Our government's negotiating team worked incessantly to gain the release of those Ukrainian prisoners.

Nothing happened for several months. But suddenly, on August 29, Russian media leaked a story saying that the Ukrainian captives were already on their way home. In a moment of euphoria, the just-appointed Ukrainian general prosecutor shared the news flash on social media. Although he had been appointed just that day, journalists, understandably, perceived him as an official who was confirming something that had already happened. This turned out not to be the case. TV stations dispatched journalists and camera crews to all the airports in Kyiv to meet the returning captives. Anonymous Telegram channels, a preferred method of distributing disinformation among the Russian tradecraft set, embellished the report of the prisoners' release with concocted details, citing sources that did not exist. By morning there was complete information chaos. Relatives cried into their phones and asked that they be allowed to meet with the returning heroes as soon as it could be arranged. Social media was abuzz with ecstatic talk of their return—how could one not believe in the news when everyone was writing about it?

We realized that this was yet another cruel Russian maneuver, just as journalists' inquiries began to pour into the government's press office. Russia aimed to show how fragile our information space was and how ill-equipped our new leadership was to deal with the unconventional, digital warfare machine it had been perfecting for a decade. Unfortunately, in this instance, it succeeded. This disinformation had raised the stakes yet again, placing us in a terrible position with our citizens as we tried to explain the inexplicable. By this feint, Russia had gained crucial leverage, allowing it to raise the price for releasing the prisoners. Having to dampen expectations in Ukraine worked against us at the negotiating table.

Ukrainians had been played for fools, but few were willing to admit falling for the trap. Disappointment did not set in at once, but it did slowly transform into public animosity toward the Office of the President.

The morning after this false alarm, I opened my email account and got the shocking full picture of how far and wide the hail of disinformation had spread. And there was more disinformation to come. There was a second false alarm on the evening of September 6. A Twitter account created by someone called "Zelenskyy" disseminated another false announcement of the prisoners' return. Piling on, pro-Kremlin Interfax Russia published its own article, attributing the information to the account that had falsely claimed to be the president's.

The prisoner exchange finally did take place, a real exchange this time, on the afternoon of September 7, 2019. The nation of Ukraine breathed a sigh of relief. Many in the media forgot about the insults they had previously lobbed at Zelenskyy and thanked the president for what he had done.

The prisoner exchange of 2019 was the first of many dramatic events to come that proved Zelenskyy's worth as a leader. The words he spoke before his election were true: he would stand with the people of Ukraine to the best of his ability. Zelenskyy had succeeded principally because of his steadfastness and discretion. Because of the undisputed success of the prisoner exchange, the possibility of a negotiated peace for the conflict in Donbas began to circulate.

By the end of April 2020, Zelenskyy had already arranged the return of a total of about 150 Ukrainian prisoners captured by Russia via several exchanges. He'd managed to achieve this in part thanks to his teams' development of sophisticated communications with the press, the public, and their diplomatic counterparts. Zelenskyy learned his lesson: today's world requires a full portfolio of options in response to disinformation. Simply remaining silent on any issue crucial to the public was not advisable, unless there was first a full consideration of its impact on press relations and how it would influence our people and the world. But he also learned that careful, selective secrecy made sense when handling certain major problems.

Zelenskyy grew fond of receiving raw data from various people within his orbit as president, gathering and analyzing that information for himself and then very often coming up with a decision that no one else had thought of. In a culture like Ukraine's, one playing host to a generational shift from oligarchy to democracy, it was crucial to do so in order to leave behind old assumptions about our people and capabilities. It was a lesson that would serve him well after the Russian invasion in 2022.

We in the press office had just breathed our first sighs of relief when news began to leak about Donald J. Trump's dramatic attempt to extort the Ukrainian president in an arms-for-dirt deal. Trump had asked Zelenskyy in a call on July 25, 2019, "to do us a favor." According to the transcript of the call with Zelenskyy, Trump wanted him to make an announcement that Ukrainian authorities were launching an investigation into the connections between Burisma, a Ukrainian oil company, and one of its board members, Hunter Biden. Hunter was the son of Joe Biden. The elder Biden had recently announced his candidacy for U.S. president and become Trump's most likely opponent in the upcoming 2020 election.

I'd learned from my sources in early August 2019 that the United States was planning to freeze $250 million in annual military aid to Ukraine. I immediately made an effort to alert the president's adviser on international relations, Andriy Yermak, about the seriousness of this issue (Yermak would later become Zelenskyy's second chief of staff). Yermak was unaware of this threat on the promised aid, and my attempts to convince him of the need to act quickly did not generate the scale of response needed. The $250 million in annual U.S. military aid had been provided to Ukraine since 2014. It had come in response to Russia's annexation of Crimea and its attack on Donbas. Ukraine relied on the U.S. aid to support its fight against Russia and Russian-backed separatists in the eastern region of Donbas.

The international media later claimed that Trump was trying to arrange a quid pro quo deal: the aid would be released only under the condition that Ukraine publicly announce it would be starting an investigation of Joe Biden's son. Trump apparently didn't seem to care or know what the U.S. aid was being used for—that it supported Ukraine's position as a defender of Europe and the Western world's interests at Russia's border. It looked like he simply sought to destroy support for Biden, the Democratic front-runner. We in Ukraine were, frankly, dismayed by the prospect of such an unexpected withdrawal of support from an important ally. But at the same time, the confusion and infighting that had been sown by Russia's disinformation campaigns concealed the full import of the situation. So nothing was done on our end; no one acted on President Trump's request to start an investigation of Hunter Biden, but no one made an effort to ensure that Ukraine would receive the already appropriated U.S. aid, either.

I was not present during the infamous conversation between Zelenskyy and Trump, but I know that the Ukrainian president was taken aback by the White House's subsequent decision to make the transcript of that call public. No one asked for the Ukrainian side's permission; we were simply informed that the transcript would come less than an hour or two before its release. Immediately, the press in the United States—and else-where—erupted. I was besieged by messages, calls, and questions from press all over the world.

Meanwhile, Zelenskyy, deeply annoyed about having his private conversation broadcast to the world, refused to comment on the issue, seeking to walk a tightrope between the two bitterly opposed parties in the United States: those who argued that Trump was tying U.S. aid to a Hunter Biden investigation as part of a political quid pro quo, and those who said this was not the case and that the two issues were not linked.

Crucially, the second group was in power at that time in the United States and was the only side who could release the aid. The situation was precarious. Zelenskyy's silence at that time, in my opinion, was the right decision. It was a hard thing for Ukraine, whose national image was one of self-reliance and strength, to have to plead for aid to support our military. Russia's annexation of Crimea and its war in Donbas had placed us in exactly that position.

Globally, discussion of the Ukrainian aid question made things sound simple: Trump had tried to place his finger on the scale. He wanted to use Ukraine's voice as if it were his own. He wanted to soil the reputation of his political opponent by generating a story his constituents wanted to hear—that Joe Biden was somehow corrupt because of his son's business dealings in Ukraine.

But locally, things were more complex. Ukraine's feelings on the matter of Hunter Biden's supposed corruption were irrelevant. Did he deserve investigation? Did it matter? From our perspective, no. He wasn't even Ukrainian. What mattered was placing ourselves in a position to retain the crucial military aid that helped us resist Russian aggression. But we also wanted to respect the United States' election process—and besides, it was quite conceivable that Hunter's father, Joe, might soon become the next president, so it was certainly not in our interest to make an enemy of the United States. It was a trusted ally, one that has since provided us with crucial military support. Without the subsequent military and financial assistance to Ukraine from the United States during the Biden administration—and from many other allies—we could not have withstood the Russian onslaught in 2022.

This international scandal drew quite a lot of attention. The U.S. Congress convened hearings to impeach Trump over his attempted extortion. Ukraine appeared in the headlines across all the major international media, unfortunately presented as a victim of its longtime ally. President Zelenskyy was not pleased with the way Ukraine was being portrayed, but Trump's role in the matter crowded out all our attempts to change the narrative. And, in the end, a package of $400 million in U.S. military aid was released to Ukraine, so we did not suffer financially.

Zelenskyy never did get an official White House invitation during Trump's presidency, as Trump had promised, but he did finally meet him in person. It was at a bilateral session during the meeting of world leaders at the United Nations in New York, in September 2019, and was meant to clear the air after the release of the transcript of their call.

I was in the delegation at those talks, listening intently to their exchange. But the subject of the scandal simply did not come up at all. It was as if it had never happened. It made sense, perhaps, that the transcript of the phone conversation was published beforehand, to prevent the comments themselves from becoming the focus of the meeting. The leaders discussed ordinary issues of mutual relations, and Ukraine was assured of U.S. support in defending against a Russian invasion of Donbas. And although Trump praised Zelenskyy's efforts in fighting corruption and made a point in saying that Zelenskyy's own reputation was impeccable, he kept bringing up corruption in Ukraine for no reason, which annoyed Zelenskyy, as the government had already made significant progress in rooting it out.

One person from our team, who dealt with Ukraine-U.S. relations, believed all along that President Zelenskyy should have promised to start an investigation to curry favor with the Trump administration (I will not mention the person's name, as this one fact can change his life). And on our plane ride back to Kyiv, that same person also claimed that the discussions we had just concluded had not gone well. Zelenskyy came up to him, smiled, put his hand on his shoulder, and said, simply, "It's okay."

With that, Zelenskyy closed the subject of the American scandal for his team. And he was right. That scandal didn't change anything in our relationship with the United States, and we succeeded in avoiding being drawn into that country's bitter political fight. That adviser eventually left the administration, and we returned home to face the next media uproar that would consume our attention and distract from our goals.

Inside Ukraine, the scandal did not make much of an impression—certainly not as much as it did in the United States. News of Trump's impeachment trial and its Ukrainian dimension slipped through from faraway America, but it had little impact on the average Ukrainian. Zelenskyy's comment about it in an interview summed up his feelings and the country's as a whole: "I think everyone in Ukraine is so tired about Burisma. We have our own country. We have our independence, we have our problems and questions."

The first time Zelenskyy commented on his now famous conversation with Trump was accidental, during an interview with four journalists from Germany, Poland, France, and the United States later that year. At the end of the session, a journalist from *Time* magazine asked a question about Trump. Zelenskyy answered, "Look, I never talked to the President from the position of a quid pro quo. That's not my thing. . . . I don't want us to look like beggars. But you have to understand. We're at war. If you're our strategic partner, then you can't go blocking anything for us. I think that's just about fairness. It's not about a quid pro quo. It just goes without saying." That modest answer helped place Zelenskyy on the cover of the December 16, 2019, issue of *Time* magazine.

All that fall, we had been intently focused on changing Ukraine's relationship with Russia. After the Sentsov prisoner swap, active negotiations began on reviving talks between the leaders of Ukraine, Germany, France, and Russia to achieve peace in Donbas. Our country was inundated with false, contradictory claims about Zelenskyy being both pro-Russian and, at the same time, overjoyed about the return of the prisoners. This information assault had the effect of raising Ukrainians' empathy for their young charismatic president (Zelenskyy was forty-one years old at the time), who was about to go head-to-head with the aging Russian dictator (Putin was sixty-seven) at the upcoming Donbas peace talks. This war had been going on for almost six long years, taking the lives of thousands of our Ukrainian defenders now buried in graveyards all around the country. Finding a resolution to the conflict was of the utmost importance. We all wanted to end the war, end the human toll it exacted, and heal our country's wounds.

With this nuanced approach—and with a change of communication strategies after Zelenskyy's first chief of staff resigned in spring 2020—our relations with journalists and the media began to improve. Within the Office of the President, whatever the leadership's policies were, there were now people responsible for communications who were authorized to speak, and the media began to get feedback on most events that were worth reporting. The Office of the President learned to communicate without divulging secrets, smearing opponents, or employing fake news. This sounds simple in hindsight, but it took many internal fights to change the culture that had persisted in Ukrainian leadership for years. And although there remained a great many communication challenges, the staff changes in the Office of the President yielded positive results.

Back in 2019, before the elections, Zelenskyy's team had worked hard to transform his image from that of a comedian to the political leader the world knows today. In addition to clips from his popular *Servant of the People* TV series and many video addresses, there was a campaign ad in which Zelenskyy spoke over footage showing America's "great communicator," President Ronald Reagan, in hopes that the Reagan magic would rub off on him. Zelenskyy's political consultants wanted him to emulate Franklin D. Roosevelt's fireside chats—radio addresses given by FDR during the Great Depression and World War II—but Zelenskyy rejected the idea.

After the Russians invaded in 2022, however, during the war, without a fireplace and not necessarily in the evening, Zelenskyy would record similar short ten-to-twelve-minute addresses to the Ukrainian people to quell rumors, to explain his policies directly to his fellow citizens, and to raise everyone's spirits. Unshaven, with bags under his eyes, and with a bleary look, he forgot to project charm, but this made him even more appealing. He spoke about what was essential, what was important to everyone, instilling confidence in times of despair and uncertainty.

CHAPTER 7

The Negotiator

Politics is like bad cinema—people overact, take it too far. When I speak with politicians, I see this in their facial expressions, their eyes, the way they squint. . . . I look at things like a producer. I would often watch a scene on the monitor, and the director and I would yell, "Stop, no more, this is unwatchable! No one will believe this!" It's the same here, only here I don't have the right to yell. I don't have the right to say "Stop! I don't believe all your promises!"

—VOLODYMYR ZELENSKYY

(INTERVIEW, *NEW YORKER*, NOVEMBER 4, 2019)

I first saw how Volodymyr Zelenskyy negotiated with foreign leaders on June 4, 2019, in Brussels, my second day on the job as press secretary. Like many, I had wondered how this man, whose considerable expertise came in business, not politics, would conduct himself in this setting. I was genuinely and pleasantly surprised. He was prepared, he knew what he was talking about, and he said all he needed to say and little more. He'd arrived with notes and later just put them aside as if he no longer needed them. No one in Brussels knew what to make of him at first, with the exception, perhaps, of loyalists of former president Petro Poroshenko, who had many contacts in Europe and had gained a reputation as being pro-European. They tried to present Zelenskyy in an unfavorable light even before he arrived in the EU capital. Moreover, the Ukrainian opposition had spread fake news in the media about his supposedly pro-Russian leanings, trumpeting his close association with one of Ukraine's most powerful oligarchs, Ihor Kolomoyskyy, who had a controlling interest in the TV channel that aired *Servant of the People.*

Zelenskyy was very conscious that at this point, making his debut as a leader on the international scene, he needed to present himself as a politician and a patriot. Deferring to his more experienced counterparts in Brussels was not natural for him; his entire being rejected it. In the years I worked for him, he regularly requested that any traces of self-pity or pathos be removed from his texts and speeches. During this particular visit, President Zelenskyy used every means he had to show he was there not in the guise of a guest but rather as a reliable partner, if not a friend. He knew that considerable macroeconomic assistance to Ukraine (1.2 billion euros) hung in the balance, so he wanted to demonstrate to the group that he would be a worthy steward on behalf of Ukraine. In addition to the aid, Zelenskyy also sought to secure agreements on free air rights (the right to fly across an airspace) with the entire EU bloc and increased trade activity between Ukraine and its EU neighbors to the west.

Negotiations at events like this were usually carried out through interpreters in the official languages of the countries and international organizations represented at the table. With rare exceptions, President Zelenskyy spoke in Ukrainian, with interpreters connecting him to other leaders speaking in English, French, German, Arabic, Hebrew, Japanese, and so forth. One of the European commissioners, a Latvian, knew Russian. As Latvia was a part of the USSR for fifty years, almost every Latvian knew or understood Russian, just as Ukrainians or any other post-Soviet nationality did. Zelenskyy saw an opportunity to connect through shared language rather than the stilted communication that often results from live interpretation and translation. It was the chance to create an understanding between them, an intangible connection. Language, after all, is not merely a means of communication. Shared language is a sign of a shared history, a common past, and a set of common values to call upon. In Russian, the two sides' interaction became noticeably friendlier, as they easily understood each other and were able to speak more freely, even with warmth. Toward the end of the conversation, they were calling each other by their first names.

There were still disagreements about some issues, but the Latvian did leave wholly convinced that Zelenskyy would stand up for a European Ukraine in the future. Poroshenko, meanwhile, remained a thorn in Zelenskyy's side, as he attacked the new government's efforts and Zelenskyy himself with disinformation across all his media channels, undermined their attempts to establish good relations, and even bankrolled demonstrations against government decisions, sometimes even those that were adopted during Poroshenko's own presidency.

But rather than dwell on Poroshenko's attacks, Zelenskyy deliberately focused on the importance of institutional continuity, one of the most significant hallmarks of a strong state. He realized early on that his primary job was to become the embodiment of Ukraine as a fully independent, sovereign state. He was always respectful to his fellow representatives, but at the same time, he would not accept talk that belittled Ukraine's sovereignty or the importance of the ongoing situation on its eastern border with Russia. He would reiterate his arguments again and again, often animatedly, using new vocabulary and introducing additional support for his belief that capitulation to Russia's expansionist policies was not an option.

Olena Zelenska, who knew Zelenskyy better than anybody, always said that her husband was persistent. This was the truth. He was relentless in his defense of Ukraine's values. One day he spent two hours instead of the scheduled one with the prime minister of Italy to negotiate the release of Vitalii Markiv, a Ukrainian National Guardsman who had been unjustly imprisoned for the death of journalist Andrea Rocchelli in the midst of the Russian conflict with Ukraine. He was tireless in repeating his arguments in the negotiations during the Normandy Format talks in Paris. Invincible persistence and an enterprising attitude about achieving his goals were embedded in his character. This is what helped Zelenskyy become a successful businessman and formed him as a politician.

Many politicians choose inaction as a means of self-preservation. They fear action because deviation from the status quo, no matter how pure in intent, could fail and cause a backlash. But in some cases, as Zelenskyy would soon learn, inaction could precipitate far larger problems.

June 21, 2020, was a very bad day. Maksym Kryvosh, a man

who'd styled himself as "Maksym the Bad," took twenty people hostage in Lutsk, a city in western Ukraine. Among them were children, the elderly, and pregnant women. As we watched the situation play out from afar and planned Ukraine's response, I couldn't help but be reminded of my own childhood. Those hostages looked like me, like the passengers on one of those old buses I'd taken as a child from village to village. The buses were freezing cold in the winter and stuffy in the summer, with the smell of gasoline permeating them as we rode.

Kryvosh was armed with guns and explosives. Moreover, he claimed he had planted additional explosives—land mines— throughout the city. It all sounded and felt like the script for a Hollywood B movie. The madman demanded that a host of officials and law enforcement personnel make a statement in which they admitted to being terrorists, and that Zelenskyy himself promote *Earthlings*, a film about human cruelty to animals. Maksym the Bad was a native Russian who had served eight and a half years in prison for robbery and was known to beat his wife, according to media reports. He held the terrified hostages for almost an entire day. Meanwhile, Zelenskyy was attending a prearranged event with Simonetta Sommaruga, the president of Switzerland, who was visiting Ukraine. It was the first visit by a head of state since the COVID-19 lockdown.

During the day, Zelenskyy took several intermissions in order to monitor the hostage situation. Negotiators had already been in Lutsk for hours, working to bring the standoff to a conclusion. But now Maksym had a new demand: that Zelenskyy himself come to Lutsk to see him. This was of course never seriously considered, but it did create an opening. Negotiators promised Maksym that Zelenskyy would come, but in fact, a Ukrainian

Special Operations Forces team would appear instead. The team would pretend to be a TV crew, overpower Maksym, and free all the hostages after arresting the terrorist. But the plan was not carried out.

Instead, the president finally reached for the phone himself, dialed the number of the hostage taker, and immediately made some headway. "Thanks to a conversation between President Volodymyr Zelenskyy and a man who calls himself Maksym the Bad, and who is holding a bus full of people in Lutsk, three persons have left the vehicle and are now free. The president continues to monitor the situation," read the message we quickly distributed to the media when he had finished.

Since the situation was not yet fully resolved, and Zelenskyy had made a promise to the terrorist, he immediately set to work on a short video advertisement for the film *Earthlings*. Earlier, several other people had tried to negotiate with the terrorist by phone and were able to keep Maksym the Bad on the line for less than a minute or even just a few seconds before he hung up. However, he stayed on the line with Zelenskyy for more than ten minutes when the president called. Although it took all evening, eventually Maksym fulfilled his side of the bargain, and all the hostages were freed. The release was shown on television. The terrorist was arrested, and no violence was used. Then the president deleted the advertisement he had made for the movie and went home. Zelenskyy had done his job on a difficult day.

But the hysteria surrounding this crisis did not subside. The opposition accused the president of surrendering to the terrorist. In fact, this was a case when the head of state had assumed responsibility, used restraint, and succeeded despite the risk of political backlash. Several of Zelenskyy's rivals decided they could raise their own approval ratings at the expense of the president by repeatedly appearing on camera and criticizing his handling of the affair.

We in the government's communications office urged the president to explain to people, in his own words, what had happened. His voice was far stronger than any of his opponents'. An explanation of the precise actions he took to free those hostages without any bloodshed would overpower the communication value of any of the attacks against him.

These kinds of moments stay with you. We returned to the office once more, finished work at 1:00 a.m., wrote up the news, and went home. I still remember Zelenskyy's statement after the hostages were freed: "I considered these steps obvious: we would do everything in our power if we could accomplish something without storming the bus, if we could avoid risking the life of even a single person. These are the principles I live by, have lived by, and will live by—to become the president but remain a human being. We are not fighting for ratings; we are fighting for life."

To be sure, negotiating with a crazed terrorist like Maksym the Bad wasn't the same as confronting Putin. He is a KGB operative turned authoritarian thug backed by a huge cache of nuclear weapons and one of the largest armies in the world, but Zelenskyy showed the sort of moral fiber that night that Putin could never match. His statement embodied our country's heartfelt respect for human life and view of fellow citizens as people, not pawns. These are the foundational values that define us Ukrainians as a European and democratic nation. Truly strong nations value life; this alone is the secret of our indestructibility.

The early negotiations with Russia in 2022 were vastly more

complicated and perilous than anything Zelenskyy had faced before, and as of this writing, the results remain uncertain. Zelenskyy's main purpose has always been to stop the wholesale and senseless slaughter of Ukrainians and the wanton destruction of our homeland. He was not personally at the negotiations, but he was intimately involved from afar.

The first groups of negotiators from Ukraine and Russia met in Belarus and then in Turkey. Moscow initially demanded the complete capitulation of Ukraine, an early indication of Putin's lack of serious interest in ending the war. The Russians wanted Ukraine to disarm, acknowledge Russian sovereignty over Crimea, and surrender the entire territory of Donbas. They also wanted the Ukrainian government to abdicate in favor of a Russian-controlled puppet government. And finally, they called for Ukraine to "denazify." This was absurd: Zelenskyy's government included a number of Jewish politicians, and he himself had Jewish roots and Jewish family members who died at the hands of real Nazis. The demands were so extreme, no representative of the government could ever agree to them, and while plain acceptance was never on the table, Putin refused to meet Zelenskyy face-to-face to even discuss compromises.

As the fighting continued and more and more Ukrainians—and Russian soldiers—died, these negotiations devolved into a farce. A month and a half into the war, the head of the Ukrainian delegation, Davyd Arakhamia, reported that "at first there was a desire to get up from the table and leave. There were very tough ultimatums." The negotiations were difficult. Ukraine was negotiating with a terrorist state.

Both Ukrainians and our president were well aware that the main negotiator in this war was the Ukrainian army and the civilians who fought alongside it. The army had fought brilliantly against the Russian war machine and had wrought terrible damage on the Russian army. And, of course, ordinary, unarmed Ukrainian civilians blocked tanks from advancing, held out against enormous force, and protested the Russian occupation of places like Kherson, even as they were being shot at.

Russia understood only power. Moscow would negotiate and look for compromise only if it looked like Ukraine would defeat Russia. If the Ukrainian army and our people did not fight and protest, and succeed in winning, Russia would not agree even to meet at the negotiating table.

CHAPTER 8

The Power of Language

We will not allow the Russian language to be privatized or given away.

—VOLODYMYR ZELENSKYY,

VIDEO MESSAGE, MAY 5, 2021

It is difficult to understand from afar how potent the issue of language is in the ex–Soviet republics. Because of its history, Ukraine has a mixture of many ethnicities and many languages. But Ukrainian and Russian prevail as the two main languages in our country (about 76 percent of citizens speak Ukrainian as their first language and about 18 percent speak Russian as theirs, as well as a small percentage of regional languages) and have existed, for the most part, in some kind of equilibrium. In fact, many people speak both interchangeably.

Nonetheless, the discussion of language today taps into some deep-seated traumas for our people. This trauma has been repeatedly inflicted by Russia's attempts to control us with its historical prohibitions concerning our language and culture, dating back at least to the time of Catherine the Great. Few people except us, for instance, know that there have been at least forty attempts by Moscow to ban the Ukrainian language since the seventeenth century. And yet today, despite everything, most of our citizens speak Ukrainian.

Nefarious actors have turned the subject of language into a tool of political polarization. Pro-Russian politicians under the Kremlin's sway still cannot accept Ukraine as an independent country with a language of its own. Ukrainian nationalists, of course, have come at it from the other side. From their perspective, it is unforgivable not to stand up to those who question Ukraine's right to self-determination.

While our politicians quarreled over the language issues, Russian-speaking Ukrainians from Odesa spent years in the trenches in Donbas, fighting the Russians and their proxies side by side with Ukrainian speakers from Lviv. In the depths of that war, the political theater of the language debate was more evident than ever. And yet we could all see that Ukrainians were fully capable of standing together, whatever language they chose to speak.

We did not need to defend either the Russian speakers or the Ukrainian speakers. We just had to defend ourselves from those who spread hatred and discord. If there was a failure among Ukrainians to understand one another, it was not because of language but because of political ambitions. The matter of which language you spoke was exploited as a symbol of political chauvinism.

Among the many expats who settled in Kyiv after the Revolution of Dignity, there was a rather progressive way of thinking about the Russian language in the context of Ukrainian society: we needed to free the Russian language from Russia's monopoly and use it ourselves. After all, Russian differed between and within various countries, from one place to another, just as English did. Even someone who didn't know English could distinguish between American and British English by the accent and choice of particular words, and though Australian and Indian English have similar phonetic forms, their intonations are very different. Microsoft already offered versions of its Russian programs and digital keyboards: there was "Russian (Ukraine)," "Russian (Moldova)," and even "Russian (Azerbaijani Cyrillic)," along with plain "Russian." The world had simply divided up the Russian language, while some Ukrainians built a new identity by rejecting everything written, or spoken, in Russian.

It would be absurd for Ukrainians, for example, to disown Mykola Hohol, the famous author of short stories, novellas, and plays, because he felt compelled to write his masterpieces in Russian. Hohol was born in Ukraine, wrote about Ukraine, and, on his trips abroad, referred to himself as a Ukrainian. He was a Ukrainian intellectual, but because he wrote in Russian and because of his literary importance, Russia has appropriated this author for itself, under the name of Nikolai Gogol. It would likewise be hard to ignore the fact that Taras Shevchenko, known by Ukrainians as the "Father of the Nation" and revered for his poetry in the Ukrainian language, had also written some prose in Russian. At least Shevchenko is not considered to be a Russian author. He devoted his life to struggling against the Russian empire and celebrating Ukrainian culture in etchings and oil paintings as well as in his poems. Shevchenko was arrested on charges of supporting Ukrainian independence and sent into exile in 1847. In 1857, after years of harsh penal servitude, he was granted his freedom by the tsar, only to die four years later.

Working with Zelenskyy, I observed that he was the first president who did not disguise the fact that Russian was his native language. Nonetheless, he had enormous respect for Ukrainian and spoke the language fluently. As president of Ukraine, he used Ukrainian in most negotiations and telephone calls, in interviews, and in speeches. But his objective was far more ambitious than favoring one or the other of these languages. He wanted to turn our knowledge of more than one language into an advantage, and like those expats, he wanted to deprive Russia of its claim on the Russian language. He also wanted to stop making the speaking of Russian in Ukraine a political issue.

Zelenskyy made one very important address in Russian before the 2022 invasion. On February 5, 2021, he spoke in Russian to explain the shutdown of three television channels owned and fully controlled by Viktor Medvedchuk, a Ukrainian politician and close ally of Putin. Zelenskyy deliberately delivered this address in Russian, the more precisely and clearly to explain his decision to those who listened to Russian propaganda. "Endless streams of lies in the Russian language, especially lately, have been poured into people's ears. And I will debunk these lies in the Russian language by truth in the Russian language," Zelenskyy began in a speech delivered from his office. "A language that, according to one party and one country, has been severely oppressed in this country. The language spoken by many of our frontline military, defenders of Ukraine, who defend us against the 'defenders' of that same Russian language that has been so badly 'oppressed.' So badly oppressed that they need to come to us with tanks."

Zelenskyy was referring to a popular story in Russian propaganda, which said that Ukrainians were oppressing Russian speakers. The Russians used this fiction to justify the occupation of Crimea, the invasion of Donbas in 2014, and their large-scale war in Ukraine in 2022. Their TV personalities, experts, and online bloggers relentlessly maintained that these actions were a "defense" of the Russian-speaking population against the Ukrainian-speaking "Nazis." And so these supposed Russian "defenders" raped, tortured, and killed innocent civilians and looted their homes under the guise of that propaganda.

That speech by Zelenskyy at the beginning of 2021 was very harsh and brave. It was dramatically different from every other official speech. It could have fallen flat. But Zelenskyy had enormous support after closing those three channels. Many knew these were not independent media outlets but Russian propaganda instruments. The lies were so concentrated, the Russian narratives so strong, that despite the controversy surrounding the decision to shut down the channels, the European Union and United States supported it. And by speaking in Russian, Zelenskyy showed that he was not going to allow Russians to privatize this other language of Ukraine: it was also his language, the native language of his parents and his children.

My mom and dad are also Russian speaking, just like the majority of inhabitants of southern Kherson, which lies far closer to the border of Russia than many other parts of Ukraine. But it sounds different from the Russian of Moscow or Saint Petersburg: my parents' way of speaking has the distinctive stress and phonetic elements that make it easy to recognize Khersonians when they speak in Russian.

I am the only one in my family who speaks Ukrainian as my

native language. This is purely by chance, the result of several circumstances. Even though my parents never expected it would turn out this way, that's how it is. I was born when they were still students. As they had to live in a student hostel in Zaporizhzhia until they completed their degrees, I spent my first years in Oleksandrivka, a village in Kherson province, where I lived with my maternal grandparents. In Ukrainian villages, the language was so rich. There was an incredible mélange, full of energy, of freedom and wisdom, of practicality and wit. Ukrainian phonetics interspersed with Russian words, Ukrainian expressions, proverbs, and organic neologisms. Was it Ukrainian? Russian? It was neither one nor the other—or perhaps it was somewhere in between.

After my parents finished their studies and we all moved to the city of Kherson, I entered a kindergarten with only Russian-speaking children. I literally could not understand what the other children were saying. My parents wanted me to know both languages, and my mom, in particular, insisted on raising me as a bilingual child. Later, I learned to understand Russian because everyone around me spoke it, but I still couldn't speak it myself. I spoke in the local dialect and stuck out like a sore thumb throughout my time in kindergarten. It took me years to master Russian, but I now speak it so well that people never know it is not my first language.

Things were a bit better after I entered elementary school in 1991, the year the USSR imploded and a new, independent Ukraine came into being. I still didn't understand the complexity of everything that was going on, but I clearly recall that at home we discussed this issue of language a lot as we were deciding on which school I should attend: The first Ukrainian-language school in Kherson? Was it a good idea to send a child to a school where Ukrainian would be spoken? Would it make things easier for me in the future? Would Ukraine be a Ukrainian-speaking country?

At the time, things were in flux. Russian had been the official language of Ukraine during the Soviet era, though many people in the western part of the country had continued to speak Ukrainian at home and among themselves. But after Ukraine declared independence, Article 10 of its new constitution declared that Ukrainian was the state language. Russian and other languages were also protected by law, but Ukrainian would predominate.

The grown-ups kept talking about it, full of doubts about what to do. They were confused enough already and didn't even know how to manage their own lives. They hadn't spoken about any of this in decades. They had grown accustomed to living according to the strict rules of the USSR, where the choice of which language to speak, and where, was not a question to be answered by citizens. It was imposed from above, by the government, and followed. Finally, the decision was made in favor of the Ukrainian-language school.

Meanwhile, in first grade, we dressed up in national costumes and wore wreaths of flowers as headdresses. My aunt, who was a teacher of Ukrainian language and literature in one of the villages in Kherson region, taught me the poetry of Ukraine's national poet, Taras Shevchenko, who was born a serf and eventually became a renowned artist and public figure, an indelible symbol of the rich and dynamic Ukrainian culture. I memorized one of his most beautiful poems to perform for my first-grade teacher on her birthday. I stood in the middle of the class and recited by heart a fragment of "A Dream," which was far too deep for a child my age:

We fly . . . I look—the dawn has come,
The sky's edge bursts ablaze;
In shady glades the nightingales
Sing out the new sun's praise.
The breezes softly, lightly wake
The steppelands from their dreams;
About the coulees, by the lakes
The willows shimmer green. *

After I finished, my teacher clapped her hands and later told my mother how beautifully I had recited. Then she gave our class a question that I was unable to find an answer to for many years: Why do people in France speak French, and in England, English, but in Ukraine—Russian?

Sometime in the middle of the year, I heard my parents saying to my aunt and my grandma in our beautiful, God-given dialect that I was the only one in school speaking Ukrainian outside class. I felt proud, not because I considered myself a great patriot or understood that this was important for the country. Rather, this was a kind of consolation for me in childhood, because I made few friends and many classmates ignored me.

When I was promoted to fifth grade, that same first-grade teacher couldn't decide whether to give me an A or a B in Ukrainian. Because of my obvious ability, I felt sure my grade would be "excellent." But at the last moment, my teacher hesitated and, after convincing herself that a B would motivate me to study harder, gave me that mark. To my childish way of thinking, this was the height of injustice.

---

* Taras Shevchenko, "A Dream," in *Selected Poetry*, trans. John Weir (Kyiv: Dnipro, 1977).

I vowed to do better. Starting in ninth grade in a different school, I participated in every Ukrainian-language competition. I never missed a dictation and wrote hundreds of compositions and won prizes for them—never first place, but always second or third.

In the academic high school I attended, I didn't immediately get into the Ukrainian-language class I wanted to take. I had to fight for a place in that class. Perversely, even though I had graduated from the eighth grade of a Ukrainian middle school, I did not arrive with enough credits to qualify for Ukrainian studies. I was assigned to a different major in which there were fewer requirements. There I was surrounded by aspiring choreographers, musicians, artists, and journalists. All the creative people together in one class.

By the end of ninth grade, I really didn't want to transfer out of that class, but both the teacher and my parents insisted. I had won academic honors for my work, a first for someone from the "creative" class. Suddenly, I found myself thrown in with the best Ukrainian-language students, at a much higher level, where the program was more substantive and demanding. To do well there, I had to study all the time. The curriculum was at the university level and included academic English-language courses and Ukrainian-language competitions of increasing difficulty: first I represented my class, then I competed at the city level with the students from other schools. After winning at that level, I competed with students from the region, then at the national level with the best students from all over Ukraine. One assignment followed another. I worked on my assignments till late every night. My days off were filled with wrapping up unfinished work and planning for the new week. I began to understand that success came from working a lot, and I was always preoccupied with my academic work.

These years of intense study helped me perform at the highest level academically. By the time I graduated with honors from high school, I already had many awards, and the admissions committee made it easy for me to get into university. Instead of three or four exams, I was required to have only one oral interview, along with the other top graduates from other schools in Ukraine. Of the twenty high school graduates who were granted interviews instead of exams, I was the only one who passed. I still remember how nervous my mother was the night before. She asked me multiple times whether I had changed my mind, as I was under so much stress. I think she was also afraid that I would move away from home if I passed the exam. But it was too late to reconsider. I arrived and entered the room where all the examiners were seated. I was being considered for a place at the best university in the country, Taras Shevchenko National University of Kyiv, in the capital of Ukraine.

Many people told us that we would be foolish to think that I would be admitted on the strength of my record. They said there was no chance unless we bribed those in charge of admissions. We never even entertained a thought of paying bribes amounting to perhaps $1,000 or even more. My parents barely earned the equivalent of several hundred dollars per month. But I don't even know if they would have been willing to pay a bribe, providing me a chance for a new life, if they had had the money to do so. But they told me they knew I was smart enough to get in without paying a bribe. And I always remembered what my teacher once said to us: "They can't let in everyone just for money. They also need smart people to represent their university." I was determined to believe this: I would be admitted because I was smart enough and prepared enough to get in on merit.

Right after my interview, the other applicants surrounded me, the only one who had succeeded. Someone asked me what I had said to get in; another asked how much I had paid. A boy from Ukrainian-speaking Lviv in western Ukraine was particularly nasty; he did not believe that a girl from Kherson could get admitted to study Ukrainian, when someone like him, from a Ukrainian-speaking region, could not.

My parents and I survived the experience. And even though in Kherson in 1991, getting admitted to Ukrainian classes was difficult, once I enrolled at the university, Ukrainian language was considered the easiest major. I lost track of the number of people, beginning in 2003, who laughed in my face: "Studying Ukrainian in Ukraine? That hardly counts as studying!" But I did study, and I graduated with honors after writing a Ph.D. thesis on contemporary Ukrainian literature.

From my earliest years, the issue of language study had been a painful one for me. Though I was privileged to have received an advanced degree from the nation's best university, my experience was fairly unique. Unlike most of my classmates, I had grown up in a poor family, in a Russian-speaking part of Ukraine, and had chosen to study Ukrainian. I was able to get a superb free education and become successful because I worked hard and my parents supported me. But it had never been easy. I could not fully process the experience until I was able to work through a certain amount of psychological trauma. I did not completely understand myself, Ukraine, or our relationship to the Russian language until a 2014 visit to Moldova's Russian-occupied territory of Transnistria.

During that trip to Moldova, I realized that the Russian-language debate was no longer simply an abstract issue. Moldova had experienced its own "Donbas" in the early 1990s and had still not recovered from it. Back then, Russia had used the same trick in Moldova that it did later in Georgia and then in parts of Russian-speaking Ukraine. Russia incited discord over language differences in order to wrest Russian-speaking territories away from newly independent countries, turning them back into occupied territories and creating black holes in the post-Soviet space.

It worked like this: In Moscow, the government propagated the myth that post-Soviet countries oppressed the Russian language and its speakers. Then pro-Russian militias, backed by the Russian army and stoked by endless amounts of disinformation, declared that they were compelled to "defend" Russian-speaking populations by seizing those territories, despite the fact that they were part of another sovereign state. The conflict in Moldova had lasted a total of two years. It was not as bloody as the war seen in Ukraine in 2022, and it ended with the creation of the Moscow-backed quasi republic of Transnistria after a phony referendum organized by the Russians, in which, predictably, 97.7 percent of the population "voted" for its creation.

The Russian Federation manufactured these language-based conflicts and referendums in the post-Soviet countries in order to justify invading some regions in Georgia, to annex the Ukrainian peninsula of Crimea in 2014, and later to invade Ukraine's Donbas. In each case, the Russians said they were "protecting" the Russian-speaking population. And right after that, those same "defenders" stormed the territories with tanks.

Transnistria was not a country; it could not be recognized as such. In fact, it was "recognized" as a republic only by the same artificial "republics" that Russia had already created in the post-Soviet space. Transnistria was an artificial gray zone without any freedoms, human rights, economy, or future. It was fully under the control of Russia. By moving its army or its surrogates into parts of post-Soviet countries, Moscow tried to preserve its presence there, using these territories for geopolitical influence and to interfere in their domestic policies.

In 2013, a majority of Moldovans were in favor of pursuing economic ties to Russia. A year later, in 2014, after observing the Russian military invasion of part of Ukrainian Donbas, Moldovan society had shifted, with 55 percent now in favor of relations with the European Union, compared with 45 percent in favor of a customs union with Russia. And it was precisely this myth of peaceful coexistence with Russia that was destroyed by Russia's violent invasion of Donbas. In effect, Moldovans had been shaken awake from the illusion of stability, seeing now that Ukraine was a defensive bulwark for all its western neighbors, including Moldova, against a Russia with a growing appetite for aggression.

They woke up, notwithstanding the fact that Russia had inundated Moldova with propaganda and post-Soviet fears about "dangerous" Ukrainians from the start of the Revolution of Dignity. People heard these stories in the news and then spread them among themselves. Here is one story I heard from a Moldovan taxi driver: Somewhere near Bila Tserkva, a town in the greater Kyiv region, a truck driver sat at his steering wheel eating when he noticed an unknown girl staring at him. After he finished his meal and got back on the road, he realized that his gold tooth was missing, and the door of his vehicle was not completely shut.

Yes, you will say, the story is improbable and even incredibly stupid. Probably the stupidest you've ever heard. But Russia produced thousands of such stories, and each time a small number of people (and sometimes a not-so-small number of people) actually believed them. This was how the Russian "Big Lie" propaganda worked.

A second taxi driver told me another story: During the winter, a trucker had driven on a road somewhere near Kyiv. Supposedly, the highway patrol had stopped him and demanded money, but he had none. He also had no cargo. Then the policemen, after searching the vehicle and finding nothing, smashed his windshield and said next time they would do the same thing to the driver.

I asked why the driver was penniless if he had already sold his cargo, and why the Ukrainians would smash his windshield. I always asked these kinds of questions whenever I heard such idiotic stories. But the driver replied, "I don't know. I was told this by the accountant of the company where the truck driver worked, and that means it's credible." I tried to suggest that perhaps there was a better explanation: perhaps the broken windshield could be explained by some "adventures" the driver had not wanted to admit to his boss. The taxi driver didn't disagree with my suggestion, but it was clear that he had never considered that the simplest alternative explanation was more likely to be true.

The taxi driver supported integration between Moldova and the European Union. But he was still unable to overcome his fear of dangerous Ukrainians. Russia has always been adept at instilling fear, the strongest of human emotions.

And if one feels afraid in Chișinău, the capital of Moldova, it's unlikely that anyone would feel differently in the TMR (Transnistrian Moldovan Republic). During the almost thirty-year history of its so-called independence, this incomprehensible pseudo country of paradoxes had brought up entire generations of people who saw and heard nothing except Russian propaganda.

By 2014, in the TMR, there remained only eight schools, where there was an ongoing struggle to retain the Latin alphabet in teaching. The aggressors in Transnistria were demanding a transition to Cyrillic, the alphabet in which the Russian language is written. And they used fear tactics to enforce their demands. Kids learning Moldovan in Cyrillic is the same as people learning English in Cyrillic: an alphabet in which nothing in that language has ever been written. As a consequence, this "education" left these kids virtually illiterate.

Such "education" was a great tool of control in this territory: it was incredibly difficult to escape from the region with nothing but the knowledge of this half-baked language. Nonetheless, since the Russian invasion in the early 1990s, the population of the TMR had shrunk by a third, from 750,000 to half a million. The majority of those remaining were old people, dooming the population to shrink even further.

A Transnistrian schoolgirl named Liza, whom I met during a recess near her school, told me that when she spoke Moldovan in public places, even if people understood her, it was unlikely they would respond. On September 1 and May 31—at the beginning and at the end of the school year—the children sang their national anthem in the company of OMON, the special units of the Russian National Guard. The unwritten rules of the KGB were flourishing in Transnistria.

Fifteen-year-old Liza, speaking frankly, said that she didn't want to cause problems for her parents. She understood that her family was a minority without rights. She yearned to leave this gray zone, this pseudo republic in the center of Europe, and dreamed of becoming a journalist one day.

On the other hand, her classmate Kristina did not intend to leave Transnistria. She knew nothing about Europe but had a lot to say about Russia. "It is a very developed country, both economically and gastronomically," said the tenth grader, describing the fantasy that Russia had tried to make everyone in Transnistria believe for the past two dozen years.

About half the pupils in the class were inclined to agree with Liza; the other half supported the pro-Russian position. What I found most interesting, however, was that these children felt no ideological aggression toward each other. They didn't even think about war or defending their national interests. My impression was that they had lost their ability to see how unacceptable their circumstances had become.

This is how I would explain the attitude of twenty-nine-year-old Vadim, who was brought up in Transnistria. It was from him that I first learned that in his native town, Dubossary, there were no job opportunities; the lone movie theater, destroyed in the 1990s, had still not been rebuilt; children had nowhere to go; and the only tourist attraction was a local liquor store. But Vadim, a taxi driver who commuted to work in Chișinău every other day, saw nothing wrong with this. He was more troubled by the fate of the grannies who could not live on their miserly pension of 700 lei (approximately $49) in right-bank Moldova. There, he said, winter heating alone cost 1,200 lei (approximately $86) a month, a fortune compared with the 100 lei (approximately $7) it cost in Transnistria. Transnistrians perceived this as solid evidence of Russia's support. And perhaps there, in the pro-Russian enclave, it was the only evidence of any attention from the Russians.

The city of Dubossary, the site of intense fighting between the Russian and pro-Russian troops and Moldovans in the Transnistria War of 1990–1992, greeted us with armed Russian "peacekeepers," their military vehicles, everywhere, and otherwise empty streets, vacant houses several stories high, and deserted factories. A billboard proclaimed: RUSSIA AND PEACEMAKERS— WE ARE FOR PEACE! We were also greeted by several rehabilitated buildings: a guarded cultural center, a church, and a school, built by Moldovans, and several rich people's houses, with many more under construction. We were told their owners were Russians but could not verify this. Dubossary remained an open wound decades after the war. Yet the inhabitants of this city were grateful to Russia for, as they understood it, a steep discount on gas.

It was unlikely they knew the real story of this "discount" on Russian gas, which was delivered to Transnistrian customers by Moldova's gas distribution company, Moldovagaz, a subsidiary company of Russian state-owned energy giant Gazprom. Chișinău, Moldova's capital, bought gas from Gazprom for all of its territory, including the left-bank Transnistrian region occupied by Russia. Chișinău could not avoid buying gas for Transnistria, because first, the Moldovan government still claimed that it was Moldovan territory, and second, the gas physically passed through Transnistria before reaching Chișinău itself. However, Transnistria's capital, Tiraspol, never paid for the gas it received. Instead, Gazprom tried to collect the money Tiraspol owed for gas from Chișinău's pockets. Over the thirty years of the existence of the pro-Russian enclave, the amount Transnistria owed had accumulated to around $8 billion. And although with the arrival of pro-European president Maia Sandu, Moldova finally started looking for ways to diversify its gas sources, Russia had blocked these attempts in every way possible. Russia is well practiced in using energy as a weapon of geopolitical influence and control. Chișinău's debts, paid or not, remained an ever-present Russian threat to the Moldovan people.

Ukraine and Moldova have much in common: a Russian threat, a shared history, and a common European future. So it was no surprise when Moldova applied for EU membership at the same time Ukraine did in 2022, right after Russia's large-scale invasion. The conflict in Transnistria was as much a problem for Moldova as Donbas was for Ukraine—these territories were a gateway for Russian influence and, ultimately, Russian incursions. Moldova accurately assessed that by not being a member of NATO or the EU, it was a likely target for Russia, right after Ukraine.

Despite their similarities, Ukraine and Moldova had four years of frozen relations, from 2016 to 2020, thanks to the pro-Russian alignment of its then president, Igor Dodon. He was one of numerous leaders of ex–Soviet republics supported by Russia in exchange for their defense of Kremlin positions.

Finally, in December 2020, Moldova elected a new, decidedly anti-Russian and pro-European president, Maia Sandu. The next year, on her first official visit as Moldova's leader, she came to Kyiv to inaugurate a new era in the relations between the two countries. Elegant, in a bright rose-colored suit, she looked even more attractive than in her photographs.

President Zelenskyy was briefed for the meeting on the various topics viewed as central to the bilateral talks: Transnistria, power supplies, common infrastructure, and, among others, language. In Moldova, language represented closeness or remoteness from the West, and Sandu wanted to request Ukraine's support for her initiatives in Ukraine's Moldovan communities.

President Zelenskyy listened attentively, asked many questions, and ultimately made proposals that would require more work for international relations and international law specialists. He suggested enacting laws that would assure cultural, humanitarian, and linguistic relations that were equally beneficial to both countries and that supported each other's language on an equal basis. Zelenskyy proposed that Ukraine and Moldova would each work to expand the teaching of the other's language in its schools: access to Ukrainian language instruction in Moldova would be equal to what was offered for the Moldovan language in Ukraine.

The agreement was decent and showed mutual respect for the rights of two international partners. With that one decision alone, Zelenskyy, who had grown up in a Russian-speaking family, did more for the expression of Ukrainian language and culture than any of the hypocritical and toothless publicity stunts of the old-school Ukrainian politicians.

Ukraine's First Lady also took a personal role in efforts to share the Ukrainian language abroad. Olena Zelenska worked with major museums across the globe to get Ukrainian added to audio guides. Thanks to her, Ukrainian is now available on guides for the Palace of Versailles, the Tower of London, and the Colosseum, and in cultural sites in Austria, Azerbaijan, Germany, Spain, Poland, Turkey, Montenegro, the Middle East, and Asia. In the United States, Ukrainian is now available at George

Washington's Mount Vernon, and her team has been working to make Ukrainian available at other major American museums.

Ukrainian is a language that is quite distinct from Russian. According to linguistic historians, Ukrainian evolved from Old East Slavic, breaking off from it over a thousand years ago. Russian is another, distinct branch of Old East Slavic. Today, linguistic experts will tell you that the Ukrainian lexicon differs by 38 percent from Russian, a bigger difference than between Spanish and Italian, which differ by 33 percent. The Ukrainian language embodies our rich intellectual and cultural history in all its diversity. In reasserting Ukrainian as our official national tongue, we also sought to reclaim that history. But Ukraine also recognizes that, along with Russian, there are various other regional languages spoken in our country, the legacy of centuries of migration, trade, wars, alliances, and border changes. Ukrainian citizens today include ethnic Romanians, Belarusians, Crimean Tatars, Bulgarians, Hungarians, Poles, Jews, Armenians, and Russians. We have been a cosmopolitan nation for a long time, and we speak with many voices.

Before the war in 2022, some politicians continued to foment division around the language debate. To attract voters, radical nationalists tried to reduce our identity to the Ukrainian language alone and divide society into first- and second-class patriots based on the language they spoke. They failed to gain much support, as it was an artificial issue that was not relevant to modern Ukraine. This political group tried to present modern identity as it was at the beginning of the twentieth century—that is, before the creation of the USSR, which had tried to transform Ukrainian culture into something rural and second-rate. But people could not erase more than seventy years of the USSR, because our grandparents and our parents were brought up in the Soviet Union. Those years were also a part of our history— sometimes joyful, more often painful—as we slowly made our way along the path toward an independent Ukraine.

Since the invasion in 2022, the Ukrainian language has received new attention around the world. Online, people have held poetry readings, and there is a team of people translating books written in Ukrainian into other languages. The Russian language, on the other hand, is suffering. It is now associated with inhumanity and cruel aggression. Russia has been accused of genocide and of being a "state sponsor of terrorism." In cyberspace, many Russian-speaking influencers in Ukraine have deliberately switched to Ukrainian, because they now associate Russian with the language of terrorism and Ukrainian with the language of freedom and democracy. What language one speaks has become a matter of principle. It is impossible to love a language if it is spoken by those who are maiming, raping, and murdering innocent people and destroying their homes. This invasion has changed everything. Instantly, it erased all the divisions that Russia and some Ukrainian post-Soviet politicians had exploited and amplified. It allowed Ukrainians to look boldly and honestly at themselves and to acknowledge who we were before and who we aspire to be today, unfiltered through anyone else's opinions.

Many influential intellectuals, writers, and bloggers who had been producing texts in Russian all their lives decided to switch to Ukrainian even during Russia's preparation for war, sometime before the invasion.

"Hi, I'm Slava, and I'm switching to Ukrainian. Taking into account the fact that for the last 38 years I spoke only Russian . . ." Slava Balbek, a Ukrainian architect and the head of the prestigious Balbek Bureau architecture firm, wrote on Instagram to his approximately sixty-five thousand followers two days before the invasion. "Today I am switching entirely to Ukrainian. I have been using it for a long time in the public sphere; now I will pull out my everyday language."

"I do not want to have anything in common with the aggressor country," wrote music reviewer Phill Pukharev on his Facebook page.

"After the Putl's speech last night, for the first time in my life I felt ashamed of speaking Russian. So I am switching to Ukrainian in social media," wrote JAXET marketing executive Andriy Tytarenko, reacting to Putin's speech in which he recognized the puppet republics of Luhansk and Donetsk and claimed that Russia was going to "protect" Russian speakers. After the Russian invasion began, the switch to speaking Ukrainian accelerated, and the transition was organic and natural.

Russia's unprovoked attack on Ukraine extinguished the possibility of nostalgia for the USSR. Putin's promotion of the concept of a Greater Russian–speaking world was nothing but an abominable pretext for mass murder and the destruction of the Ukrainian people and the society we are building as an independent, sovereign state. We want our country back. And our national language is and always will be Ukrainian.

CHAPTER 9

Oligarchs and Fake News

*There is no slavery in the world, but there is
financial slavery.*

—VOLODYMYR ZELENSKYY

(INTERVIEW, *AXIOS ON HBO*, JANUARY 23, 2021)

In September 2019, Angela Merkel had grown so concerned about the issue of Ukrainian oligarchs that she requested
a special meeting with Zelenskyy during the weeklong meeting
of world leaders at the UN General Assembly. It was early in Zelenskyy's time in office, and it had a long-lasting effect on their
relationship.

Merkel speaks Russian very well, but her modesty obliges
her to downplay that fact. The first woman to hold the post of
federal chancellor of Germany—making her the most powerful
woman in the world—Merkel was distinguished by her excep-
tional simplicity and grace. People talked about her composure
in delivering public speeches, where she always spoke plainly,

which was true, but I think the most important of all her qualities was the ability to remain a real person. This was a considerable feat for someone who had served for so long as the leader of an influential and powerful country. While some longtime leaders turn themselves into dictators to extend their power, Merkel chose to do her job for the constitutionally allowed sixteen years, all the while transforming power into wisdom, and experience into understanding. And then she stepped down.

Merkel was always capable of surprising people. She commanded the room; she made eye contact with each person she met, offering a handshake to every delegation member at high-level meetings, bestowing the gift of respect with her gaze. Greeting me among an all-male delegation the first time we met, she said, smiling, in Russian, ". . . and one woman." At the time I was pleasantly surprised and replied in English that we would remedy that situation. Merkel did not expect such a breach of protocol, but she and Zelenskyy both laughed.

To watch Merkel at the negotiating table was eye-opening. Although the details of her position about the conflict in Donbas are classified, I can at least say that she approached negotiations with real assurance. She had been trained to assimilate information quickly and be well prepared for meetings. It was evident to me that she was in her element there. Merkel was much more comfortable in negotiations than in public speaking. She had a lively interest in every detail and had mastered her brief. She did not hide her surprise if something was mentioned that she did not already know, and while always maintaining the professional demeanor of a politician, she expressed a certain kindness to individuals she liked.

I will never forget that very important meeting with Merkel, squeezed into crowded schedules during the UN General Assembly's annual meeting in 2019. The chancellor initiated it herself. We had dropped in to the Indonesian Lounge, a rather large room designated for exploratory negotiations at the UN. It was divided by sturdy partitions; the tables for different delegations were spaced so far apart that we could not even see whether there were other delegations in the room.

Merkel literally burst through the door, serious and very composed, in a bright red jacket. She quickly went around the room and shook everyone's hand and looked them in the eye, as was her habit. I was standing behind two transparent round glass tables placed against each other and certainly did not expect Merkel to reach all the way across the tables toward me. But she did, and I instantly leaned in to meet her halfway, and we had a light, but warm, handshake. This small, inconsequential moment will always stay with me, as it taught me an important lesson: no honor, position, amount of money, or accomplishment can prompt a real leader to forget how to treat another person respectfully. I don't know if this was the secret of Merkel's power and what inspired the German people's faith in her, but I suspect this aspect of her character was also part of her appeal.

We were meeting at her suggestion, and she had a question for President Zelenskyy. Back then, in September 2019, the well-known Ukrainian oligarch Ihor Kolomoyskyy had been bragging about how much influence he had over Zelenskyy. Predictably, opposition leader Poroshenko used this as an opportunity to undermine the newly elected president. Merkel was quite upset by some stories that had come to her attention, and she wanted to ask Zelenskyy about them.

This was at a time when Kolomoyskyy was unusually visible

in the media. But although none of us had anticipated Merkel's question, Zelenskyy found his bearings quickly and responded to Merkel with complete candor. He said that Kolomoyskyy had no role in the government and that not a single government official had had any dealings with Kolomoyskyy about anything, nor had anyone negotiated with him in the name of the government of Ukraine. On hearing this, Merkel's face visibly relaxed. During that short meeting in New York, what was at stake for our government was something much greater than reassuring her that Zelenskyy was not beholden to the oligarchs. At stake was the trust of the most influential woman in global politics and a key figure in the negotiations regarding Donbas. Looking over our team with an experienced eye, she could see that Zelenskyy was telling the truth and decided to trust him. He would enlist Merkel's support on many issues going forward and had acquired a strong ally in his negotiations with Russia.

Merkel was right to be concerned: oligarchs were like an invasive species, spreading their weblike influence into every area of life and suffocating everything. Even though oligarchs were not official representatives of the government, they nevertheless had accumulated a huge amount of power in their hands, owning Ukrainian resources and enterprises, influencing politicians and the financial system. Merkel understood this and condemned those who built their wealth and power through unfair, unchecked, and greedy competition. Although she commanded more power than any Ukrainian oligarch could ever dream of, she devoted it to strengthening one of the mightiest states in the world. Meanwhile, the oligarchs continued to undermine the state of Ukraine. And now Kolomoyskyy was doing just that.

After this meeting, realizing the danger of allowing rumors

to circulate unchallenged about the president's relationship with Ukrainian oligarchs in general and Kolomoyskyy in particular, I offered to draft an op-ed in Zelenskyy's name for an American newspaper to set the record straight. But Zelenskyy demurred, instead taking the advice of Andriy Bohdan, the first chief of staff of the Office of the President, who vigorously objected to the idea. To my dismay, a month and a half later Kolomoyskyy gave an interview to the *New York Times*, advocating a turn toward Russia. I was distressed to read his words in the *Times*, a newspaper whose standards I generally admire. But in this instance, it was entirely off base and misleading to allow Kolomoyskyy to comment on official Ukrainian policy. I hope the *Times* journalist who interviewed Kolomoyskyy later felt ashamed for believing that an oligarch like him could influence the president of Ukraine. I was even more distressed to learn that the *Washington Post* and the *New Yorker* also had interviews lined up with Kolomoyskyy. I wrote to the president, urging him to issue a single, simple statement: "Ihor Kolomoyskyy is not a representative of the authorities or Zelenskyy's team. He has no authority to say anything on behalf of Ukraine or the Office of the President, no positions on state affairs are discussed with him." The statement was made and apparently everyone heard it loud and clear. After that, the international media refrained from presenting the Ukrainian oligarchs as credible representatives of the country's society or policies.

Historically, the big oligarchs were allowed to play a significant role in shaping Ukraine's international image. Starting in the 1990s, after the dissolution of the Soviet Union, a few of these businessmen divided among themselves the most important sources of wealth in Ukraine, creating monopolies from former state-owned enterprises, including oil, gas, farmland, mineral extraction, and telecommunications. Periodically they would get into fights over who owned what—battles that sometimes resulted in some of them changing places on the list of Ukraine's wealthiest individuals.

The frequent and rapid changes of government in Kyiv gave the international community the impression that Ukraine was too unstable and weak to fight the oligarchs, which was mostly correct for a long time. Bear in mind that by 2020, Ukraine had gone through twenty prime ministers and their governments during the thirty years since independence. Mykola Azarov, prime minister from 2010 to 2014 during the corrupt presidency of Viktor Yanukovych, held the post the longest, for almost four years; several others warmed that chair for only half a year. It is difficult even to count up the number of ministers who have come and gone. Such instability was responsible for the institutional weakness of the cabinet; it reduced individuals' responsibility for outcomes and incentivized short-term planning.

Moreover, the oligarchs' influence wasn't limited just to the control they exerted over the airwaves, enterprises, land, or useful minerals. Their behavior also directly affected people's livelihoods. Because they had a monopoly on most businesses, the oligarchs were responsible for creating the majority of jobs in Ukraine, and they employed and cultivated relationships with the country's professional elites.

How did this complicate matters in Ukraine? The oligarchs, in response to any attempts to curb them or what they viewed as unsatisfactory decisions on the part of the authorities, would unleash floods of negative or even fake news through the most popular media platforms they controlled. They would also shut down their own enterprises in retaliatory fashion, with resulting job losses.

Because of their powerful connections, the oligarchs' hand-picked people were able to climb the corporate ladder with ease and to become successful in their fields. These same people would then enter politics, reaching the rank of minister and even the position of prime minister. But even without those tight "connections" to the oligarchy, the odds were high that whenever the oligarchs felt it necessary, they could use their considerable resources to bribe and influence most government officials.

When Zelenskyy came into office, he made numerous personnel changes. The turnover did not immediately strengthen governmental agencies and institutions, but it did create room in the government for new talent. Coming as he did from the business world, Zelenskyy wanted to implement sorely needed business-based methods of efficiency and flexibility in the public sector. He wanted to modernize the top-heavy, technologically backward, bureaucratic machinery of the state by introducing quality management practices and better communication with Ukraine's citizens. The presidential office hired an HR firm, which announced job openings and interviewed candidates, choosing the most qualified among them.

There were also organizational changes in the offices themselves to streamline how work was done. It motivated staffers to work more effectively and more productively. But at the same time, they knew that the risk of failure was quite high. There was significant turnover throughout the government, and many were afraid to make a mistake or let the new government down in their new roles. It felt chaotic at times, and some people were confused by what they were supposed to be doing. But those who were able to meet the rigorous new standards were soon promoted to positions with more responsibility. Suddenly, it became clear that hardworking, smart people with no connections could make it to the top.

It was no secret that removing the oligarchs' influence on political power in Ukraine would be difficult. For thirty years an entire system of cooperation and confrontation between the state and the oligarchy had been in place. Our parliament was filled with wealthy members who received income from dozens, if not hundreds, of businesses. Some members of parliament were themselves lobbyists who broke the laws, scorned morality, manipulated the media, and blocked reforms.

But even before Zelenskyy's election, there had been some initial, important efforts to de-oligarchize the country. Ukrainians first became familiar with the term "de-oligarchization" after the 2014 Revolution of Dignity. Everyone knew what the word meant—that we had to dismantle the power of the oligarchs—but no one had a concrete plan for how to do it.

One of the first efforts to curb the oligarchy came when the Ukrainian political leadership and international organizations took on the egregiously corrupt PrivatBank, whose majority partner was Kolomoyskyy. It was Ukraine's largest bank, and the country's entire financial system depended on its existence, and it was on the brink of insolvency because of shady lending practices. The government nationalized the bank in 2016. Kolomoyskyy left the country as a fugitive and didn't return to Ukraine until 2019. But though he lost control of PrivatBank and could not return to the country, he retained control of many other large, monopolistic companies, which continued to generate revenue, and by 2018, his assets had soared to between

$1 billion and $1.6 billion. Simply speaking, while international institutions were devising instruments to fight corruption, Ukrainian oligarchs were just as creative in figuring out ways to keep dodging accountability and to generate profits for themselves.

So although in some important ways the process of de-oligarchization had begun before Zelenskyy came to power, there was no blueprint for what to do next. Without a concrete program in place and little visible progress being made, de-oligarchization soon became an empty populist slogan. It became clear during the administration of Poroshenko, himself one of the richest men in Ukraine, that it was quite difficult to develop a transparent program of de-oligarchization.

Poroshenko, even while in office as president, owned several TV channels. He used those outlets during his presidency and after he left office as a bully pulpit, promoting his party and his political faction in parliament. He certainly did not want to destroy the system on which he and his comrades had built their businesses.

"Ukraine does not have a law on lobbying, unlike some European countries and the United States," Zelenskyy noted in a 2021 interview for *Axios on HBO*. He went on to observe that lobbying and oligarchy are quite similar in many ways—in how large financial groups and their representatives influence the adoption or non-adoption of certain bills, which then ensures a profit to these financial groups. "When they say that there are oligarchs all over the world," Zelenskyy concluded, "I absolutely agree. They are just civilized." In Ukraine, in other words, oligarchs used coercion—or money—rather than persuasion to get what they wanted.

In 2008, the combined wealth of Ukraine's fifty richest oligarchs was equal to 85 percent of Ukraine's GDP. By 2018, according to World Bank data, the combined assets of the three wealthiest individuals in Ukraine still exceeded 6 percent of the nation's GDP. This amount was roughly equal to Ukraine's entire pension fund. The oligarchy's negative impact on Ukraine's present—and its future—was evident to all. In 2018, the independent Ukrainian media outlet *Novoe Vremya* observed that the richest one hundred Ukrainians grew their wealth "12 times faster than the country's GDP is growing. And the growth rate of their fortunes has only increased over the past year." So, while Poroshenko's five-year term in office saw more reforms constraining the oligarchs than in the preceding twenty-two years, the oligarchic system remained strong. The pervasive corruption and poverty in our country were a result of the oligarchs' monopolies in every sphere, stifling competition and allowing no opening for small businesses. Their size and influence prevented Ukraine from advancing—despite all our efforts, we were still the poorest country in Europe. Foreign investors did not trust they could get a fair deal in Ukraine's anticompetitive environment, and between 2018 and 2019, our standing in world ratings declined by two points in the Corruption Perceptions Index, an important indicator for the international community.

It was clear in 2018 that the battle to free ourselves from the oligarchs still lay ahead.

One of the main reasons Zelenskyy was elected in 2019 was because the voters wanted a president who would commit finally to dismantling the power of the oligarchs. Zelenskyy and his party promised to do just that. But the political realities he faced were daunting. When Zelenskyy was sworn in, he had to make more than one political compromise to ensure that the oligarchs

would not cut his presidency off at the root. Zelenskyy understood how the oligarchs operated and was honest with himself: if
he began an internal information war with the country's biggest
TV channels all at once, the media conglomerates backing them
would have a field day attacking and discrediting him.

First he had to deal with Kolomoyskyy, who was trying to re-
gain his assets lost during Poroshenko's rule. Rumors persisted
that Zelenskyy was considering returning PrivatBank to Kolomoyskyy, but the president never seriously considered any steps
that would return the bank to him. The oligarch applied pressure through his TV channel 1+1, using it to attack Zelenskyy
and to try to sabotage his popularity ratings.

During his presidential campaign in 2019, Zelenskyy had
backed legislation intended to grant amnesty for capital accumulated under questionable circumstances—a one-time opportunity for capitalists to declare any ill-gotten gains, pay back
taxes, and receive amnesty. The idea was that money that had
been illegally taken out of the country would return, replenish
Ukrainian coffers, and stimulate new investments. Ukrainians
who had enriched themselves by doing shady business in their
country could make use of their ill-gotten gains and escape pun-
ishment. But this could be done only once. In exchange, these
businesspeople gained an opportunity to transparently reenter
the government's financial system, enjoy its advantages, and
resume their business activities in Ukraine. If they didn't accept
this offer, they would be barred from investing in Ukraine. The
measure was voted into law in June 2021, and the opportunity
was offered for a one-year period. As of January 2022, Ukrainians had declared over $40 million.

Even before the proposal to institute an amnesty for capital became public, it was attacked. Some in parliament falsely accused President Zelenskyy of being a defender of the oligarchs. Zelenskyy's position was pragmatic; he felt that recovering at least some of the money that had been spirited out of the system would be a good thing, and that eventually he could convince the wealthy that financial transparency would be better for them in the long run.

In the summer of 2021, additional legislation was introduced that specifically targeted Ukraine's oligarchs, identifying them by means of certain criteria. Then it hit them with restrictions to limit their influence, such as prohibiting them from financing political parties and from participating in large-scale privatization tenders for state property, among other things. These oligarchs were also required to declare their earnings, just like state officials, and could no longer hold off-the-record meetings with any government officials. When Zelenskyy introduced the law, the opposition was fierce. The new law, which took effect in May 2022—though it may now be delayed because of the Russian invasion—provided the first legal definition of an oligarch: a major monopolist with a fortune of over $80 million who has influence over politics and the media.

After the law was submitted to parliament, the oligarch-controlled TV channels devoted countless hours to fighting the president. They accused him of everything bad happening in the country, from the weaknesses of his team to the energy crisis. Nonetheless, the bill passed and became law on November 5, 2021.

Another example of how the government tried to intervene to curb the oligarchs' monopolistic practices became one of the biggest controversies of early 2021. That year, Spain experienced an unusually severe winter. An unexpected snowstorm caused temperatures to plunge, and within hours, news and social media showed images of snowdrifts several meters high and happy snowboarders who'd taken the metro to launching points on the snow-covered mountains.

The downside to this unexpected snow event, however, was an accompanying surge in heating costs. Very swiftly, the price of gas in Europe increased more than it had in a year. Naturally, this change in the market price was reflected in prices in Ukraine. A planned increase had already been going on for several years to raise Ukraine's rates up to the level of the world market, a measure to minimize the risk of corruption and to stabilize pricing through market competition. But even though the market approach used to price gas was correct overall and did significantly reduce the influence of the oligarchs in this sector, from the start there were some elements in that policy that contradicted the reform. For one thing, while this temporary price increase helped the economy, it was putting pressure on consumers and on the state budget. But as the Ukrainian people were paying higher prices, the oligarchs still continued making profits.

Dmytro Firtash, an oligarch in the natural resources sector best known for his dominance of the natural gas industry, controlled about 80 percent of Ukraine's natural gas supply through his group of provincial gas suppliers across the country. In sum, about thirteen million people got their gas from Firtash-controlled companies.

Firtash-controlled gas prices fluctuated from around $320 to $425 per 1,000 cubic meters, while Naftogaz, the state-owned natural gas company, sold gas for around $260. Zelenskyy explained in public statements that Firtash bought his gas from his own offshore companies and could raise (or lower) the prices for his customers whenever he wished.

Every day Firtash raked in tens of millions of dollars while individual consumers had no mechanism to shift their gas consumption from one supplier of gas to another because of Firtash's monopoly. Calculations by foreign colleagues pointed out that even if it were possible to shift public consumers over to Naftogaz, only 47 percent of them would be able to do this in 2021. It meant that high rates were the reality now, and the possibility of lowering them would not occur until several years in the future. This was a terrible situation for Ukrainians who could not afford these prices and who were always being asked to wait.

A solution was worked out with all the state agencies involved in the market. State regulation of the market price for gas was temporarily imposed, not only to lower the January prices for heating and hot water, but also to forestall an anticipated further rise to come in February. A price of around $255 per 1,000 cubic meters of natural gas was set. Just think how much profit Firtash lost as a result.

Needless to say, a wave of indignation resulted. On one side were opponents who took the opportunity to accuse government supporters of raising the rates at a time when gas rates were rising all over the globe. On another side were Firtash's flunkies, who berated the president on behalf of their embittered boss. And on a third side were international partners, who worried about a longer-term return to state control over the energy market.

Fortunately, Zelenskyy's team succeeded in conducting negotiations and explaining the essence of its decisions to the public. First, as Zelenskyy had noted before, the provincial natural gas companies, controlled by Firtash, bought natural gas from their own offshore companies. They claimed their markup was minimal, but the initial price was set not by the market but by Firtash himself, a major beneficiary. In reality, before the state stepped in to regulate the market, a single oligarch controlled a large part of it.

Later in the year, we began an information campaign to explain to Ukrainian customers how they could transition from their current natural gas supplier to another. Within a week, the provincial gas companies (those controlled by Firtash) complained that they were losing up to fifteen thousand customers daily. Firtash would now have to compete with the prices charged by Naftogaz.

It was a real victory for the government, despite all the demonstrations and negative attacks. And though in this instance the Ukrainian consumers also won, many more anti-corruption measures were needed to rescue them from the proliferation of oligarch-run businesses that were so deeply embedded in state institutions.

This fight against the energy oligarchy had another side to it. When the gas market had to be regulated for the third year in a row, it essentially meant rolling back reforms. In addition, like all oligarchs, Firtash had a talent for finding new corruption schemes when the old ones were blocked. Even after his defeat over the regulation of gas prices, still, in 2021, Firtash was the twenty-fifth-richest man in Ukraine, according to *Forbes*, with more than $400 million in assets.

"It is possible to do it, I want to do it in Ukraine," Zelenskyy said in January 2021 interview with *Axios on HBO* about getting rid of the country's endemic corruption, which felt sometimes like a game of Whac-A-Mole. "This must be accepted. It is not just a decision of law enforcement officers to imprison someone. I am not against imprisoning anyone who breaks the law. But others will come instead of these. Therefore, it is necessary to change this process at the legislative level. I believe it is possible to do so."

Not only was action needed to identify and root out corruption in businesses and in the personal financial affairs of the oligarchs themselves, but the government also had to address the destructive influence of the disinformation they were pushing. Zelenskyy explained that he would do it in two ways: one, by depriving the oligarchs of the opportunity to control TV media platforms, and two, by restricting their opportunities to influence politicians.

On February 2, 2021, Zelenskyy imposed sanctions against three television channels and their nominal owner, Taras Kozak, a close associate of the oligarch Viktor Medvedchuk, who was in turn a friend and close associate of Vladimir Putin. These television channels—112 Ukraine, NewsOne, and ZIK—were immediately taken off the air. Filled with propaganda, their programming had deviated by light-years from real journalism. They used fake news to attack every anti-oligarch reform, every effort to move toward creating a solid market economy. They peddled incendiary topics, stirring up conflicts over language and religion, and distorted every possible fact. The fingerprints of various political and financial groups were clearly visible in the content they pushed. Their messages dovetailed with those disseminated by pro-Russian bloggers, pro-Russian newspapers, and the pro-Russian party Opposition Platform—For Life (OPZZh). All this was further amplified by bots pushing the same disinformation.

The Russians were expert at this kind of fake news TV programming. A friend of mine told me that once, as an experiment, she accepted an invitation to a political talk show on the main state-owned propaganda channel, Russia-1. In Ukraine, we typically prefer not to do this, because Russian media networks like Russia-1 make no attempt to be balanced or fair in their coverage. The concept of "objective media" is nonexistent. They pretend to be open to other opinions by inviting someone on the air, but then they simply hound the person.

Knowing this, my friend still made the courageous decision to experience the Russian media operation at work from the inside. She was put on air with five other speakers, all of whom told incredible lies about Ukraine and insisted that the Kremlin was right on every issue. When she began to speak, she was interrupted by the other "experts" onstage. At times the hosts and engineers even muffled her microphone to prevent her from presenting her perspectives or defending herself against accusations. She was silenced so that her arguments would not be heard and outweigh the propaganda. After the broadcast, the hosts became nice again and invited her to dinner, then smilingly asked her not to get angry, saying, "We're just doing our job, you know."

On one occasion, the fake news TV tactics took a deeply personal turn. Russian journalists broadcast a lie that I was pregnant with the president's baby. For eleven minutes, live on Russian television, six experts discussed my nonexistent affair and pregnancy. That disinformation spread so widely throughout the former Soviet Union that I received calls from places like Belarus and Kyrgyzstan. The real target of this disinformation attack, of course, was not me, but rather the first couple of Ukraine—the president and First Lady. The story bore all the hallmarks of everyday Russian disinformation: chauvinistic, below-the-belt, personal innuendo with not a sliver of evidence or truth.

ZIK, one of those three pro-Russian Ukrainian TV channels taken off the air for broadcasting Russian propaganda, had Olena Lukash on-screen just as the network went dead. Lukash, the former minister of justice under Yanukovych, who had fled to Russia to escape responsibility for his corrupt regime, was in the middle of propagating her routine lies about the supposed banning in Ukraine of books and films in the Russian language when it happened. "Our children will never again see *The Trio from Prostokvashino* [a very popular Soviet cartoon by a Russian author]," she said. Then the screen went black. A week or two later, Zelenskyy said, "We didn't shut down our channels. We shut down *theirs*," making clear that they were Russian propaganda channels.

Taking Medvedchuk's channels off the air was a bold and decisive act. Medvedchuk was the most insolent, pro-Russian, anti-government member of the oligarchic elite, and this was the first time since the declaration of Ukraine's independence in 1991 that anyone had dared to cut the umbilical cord tying Ukraine to the Kremlin. After the Russian annexation of Crimea in 2014, Medvedchuk was put on a U.S. sanctions list. Tape recordings of Leonid Kuchma, Ukraine's second president, in 2002 quote him as saying Medvedchuk was "a KGB agent, 100 percent." Medvedchuk had a monopoly on the supply of diesel fuel to the entire Ukrainian army, as well as on coal and liquefied natural gas from Donbas and the occupied territories. Dozens of companies listed in the name of his wife, Oksana Marchenko, were registered in the Ukrainian territories seized by Russia. Of course, he also sold coal to Russia. He and Putin were friends. Putin became the godfather of Medvedchuk's daughter Darya in 2004.

It is impossible to recall another moment in Ukrainian politics when, at the halfway point in his term, a president received such a positive response to his address to the nation. "Those who routinely do business with [territories annexed by Russia in 2014], who routinely maintain ties with the illegal military units and pseudo structures in these territories—all of them represent a threat to our country. This means that our country will struggle against them, and this is also the standard we will follow," Zelenskyy stated in a video from his office. "I am obliged to act and will act, using all legal means at my disposal to neutralize such threats. Including with the help of sanctions." The closures, he explained, were in accordance with measures taken to sanction the communications combatants within Ukraine. "Let's be honest—today our leaders are getting slammed by all channels. But not all channels are sanctioned by the authorities," President Zelenskyy added. Then he talked about the propaganda war that was under way. He spoke about when television channels reported myths about land reform, alleging that Ukrainian politicians had supposedly sold off land to foreigners. He spoke about their reporting on protests over rate hikes on fuel, even as they knew full well that the pro-Russian party was paying for these protests. Finally, the president explained what was really bothering him personally: "But the main point is something else," he said. "While they are earning money from the war, they are convinced there is actually no war. To be more precise, they say it is a civil war. No, not in the sense that citizens of Ukraine and Russia are fighting each other. But that it is our domestic conflict. A quarrel. Such a small-scale civil strife. Just think, tens of thousands killed. . . ."

Just weeks later, the National Security and Defense Council levied sanctions on Medvedchuk, his wife, and his associate Taras Kozak, who carried passports from two countries, Ukraine and Russia. The sanctions blocked access to their assets, financial operations, and private airplanes.

For the first time, Russia was seeing that Ukraine had some real teeth and that it would not simply accept wave after wave of destructive propaganda. Ukraine would bite back, if attacked.

Two weeks later, Ukraine moved to sanction nine hundred miles of oil pipelines owned by a company under Medvedchuk's control, with the objective of restoring them to state ownership. A week after that, the United States introduced the first symbolic sanctions against Kolomoyskyy, while also condemning his corruption during his governorship of the Dnipropetrovsk region.

Then Zelenskyy doubled down. Following a regular session of the National Security and Defense Council, he issued a statement naming absolutely every one of the Ukrainian oligarchs:

"On U.S. sanctions on the former owners of PrivatBank. We support this decision and are working to return these assets to Ukraine. In order to bring justice to Ukraine. The major principle is that we clearly see the difference between the concepts of 'big business' and the 'oligarchic class.' The names listed here are not what is important: Medvedchuk, Kolomoyskyy, Poroshenko, [Rinat] Akhmetov, [Victor] Pinchuk, Firtash, or any other. Only one thing is important: Are you prepared to work within the law and work transparently, or do you want to continue creating monopolies, to control mass media and influence parliamentary deputies and other state officials? The first is viable, the second is over and done with," Zelenskyy declared.

Considering that all the other Ukrainian television channels were still in the hands of the oligarchs, Zelenskyy risked a lot, standing against a corrupt Ukrainian political system that, notwithstanding his decisive actions, might well have eaten him alive. In 2021, this was exactly what occurred with Akhmetov's TV channels. The richest of all the Ukrainian oligarchs had strongly opposed the presidential law on de-oligarchization, and when it was enacted, Akhmetov's TV channels exploded with attacks, some completely untrue, and the rest without much concern for journalistic ethics or balance. Only the Russian invasion stopped this bacchanalia of invective.

Once the 2022 war started, many oligarchs, including Akhmetov, Pinchuk, and Kolomoyskyy, among others, at least publicly threw their support behind the president. Poroshenko and Zelenskyy reportedly shook hands and agreed to work together. In order to provide a single message to the Ukrainian people, most Ukrainian TV channels were merged into one TV channel broadcast. Poroshenko's channels were banned.

While Ukrainians in general had celebrated the earlier shuttering of Medvedchuk's channels because they were nothing but Russian propaganda, the tight control of the media during the war, though understandable as a defense measure, drew concerns about the future of freedom of speech. In the second month of the war, the government channel was reported to have only 5 percent trust from the Ukrainian people. And still Poroshenko's channels were banned from broadcasting.

As the Ukrainian oligarchs fought with their own government, another part of the picture came into focus: an era had begun in which deep-rooted Russian influence was being challenged in Ukraine. That undoubtedly was one of the reasons for the furious Russian invasion of 2022. Putin realized that he had to invade our country and install a proxy such as Medvedchuk, or risk losing his grip on Ukraine.

CHAPTER 10

Learning to Live in a Democracy

If we want to build a democratic, civilized country,
we must follow world law. We must remain humans.

—VOLODYMYR ZELENSKYY

(INTERVIEW, *AXIOS ON HBO*, JANUARY 23, 2021)

In the video archive of President Zelenskyy's press office, there were some extremely interesting clips that hadn't ever appeared in public. We decided to preserve them: first, because the press office should keep everything, and second, because for us these video clips were filled with pleasant and amusing moments.

In one, President Zelenskyy was chatting with two elderly priests when the videographer recording their interaction broke a vase. We couldn't see the vase in the frame, but we could hear that he knocked something over and the object fell and broke. The old men looked at the videographer with surprise and indignation, but the president walked over to the broken object, bent

171

down, and picked up the fragments. It was one of those moments when we saw the president's common decency and simplicity—very important aspects of his character. And we laughed because the videographer, whose name was Vova, short for Volodymyr—the same nickname and name as the president's—was carefully filming the entire time as the president bent down and gathered up all the fragments. Vova, of course, never thought to pick them up himself.

There was another video, shot by the same videographer, from the front lines in Donbas. In February 2021, Zelenskyy traveled to Donbas with six foreign diplomats. Anka Feldhusen, the German ambassador to Ukraine, was having trouble fastening her helmet's chin strap. The president noticed this and began to help her with it. I sent that short, sweet fourteen-second video to Anka.

But there are other moments recorded only in our memory: For example, when we set out on one of our first trips to the provinces. It was like accompanying a rock star. So many people rushed over to see Zelenskyy, to join him as he walked, and, even better, to take selfies with him. They surrounded us in a tight circle, now and then shouting out the president's first name or squealing with joy. Our security team struggled as the crowd pressed in to get a look. In the midst of the crowd was a young mother with a little girl, and she was struggling to lift her up. The crowd, shoving and pushing, was pressing in hard against the child. The frightened mother was at a loss. I was trying to protect the child, who had begun to cry. Zelenskyy heard her cries and turned back. He spotted the little girl, walked over to her, and gestured to the crowd to back off, and his security detail helped out. He squatted next to the crying child and tried to calm her. The crowd stopped shoving, and the mother asked for a selfie to remember the moment.

I mention these trivial incidents only because seeing Zelenskyy in action, knowing his values and the way he views the world, made some of the characterizations of him seem ludicrous. They were, in fact, political attacks by his opponents attempting to demean or discredit him as a politician, constructing an alternative image of him online—as a coward, an arrogant jerk, or a fool.

Zelenskyy often tried to correct that image himself, sometimes offending several journalists as he accused them of writing only negative stories and putting out fake news. But he wanted to insert his own vision and his own side of the story into an information space that was immature, unregulated, and without rules or boundaries.

After he became president, Zelenskyy soon grew familiar with the use of protests as a political tool. It was easy, we found, to create a convincing picture when the people who orchestrated the protests had their own television channels and were able to cover the events from an angle that would best advance their agenda. Of course, the true motives for the protests were obscured by beautiful slogans about the struggle for justice, but many of them were less an outpouring of spontaneous, sincere sentiment than a calculated effort to influence political decisions, cancel bills, or promote some special interest. In one instance, a raucous crowd materialized, berating Zelenskyy for being pro-Russian because he reconvened the stalled peace talks with Russia. He was seeking an end to the Donbas conflict. There were no actual fights, but the protests were artificially stoked by hired rabble-rousers and filmed to make them seem enormous and violent on TV. Other times, crowds were assembled to demonstrate against bills on financial transparency, land reform, even the nonpayment of salaries by private businesses. This was rent-a-crowd politics. Often the demonstrators did not even know what they were protesting and could not explain why they had come to the rally.

Of course, not all these demonstrations were staged. There were also real protests organized by committed activists who were unhappy with one or another decision the government had made. Democracy is always accompanied by heated discussions. But unlike in Russia, the Ukrainian government did not put people behind bars for protesting.

Zelenskyy paid careful attention to what was happening at demonstrations that occurred all over Ukraine in 2020 and 2021 and what effect they had on the image of his government. He tried to discover who organized them, who financed them, the motives of the organizers, and how many people demonstrated and where they were from. How much they were paid was the least important concern to him. Most important was to find out what was real and what was orchestrated.

He was seriously concerned about the so-called tariff genocide protests opposing the rise in tariffs on gas, electricity, and heating, which hit poor people particularly hard. The protesters were stirred up by Medvedchuk, who seized on this issue to foment unrest in the country. Demonstrations were held in various parts of Ukraine.

Just like the shows on Medvedchuk's already shuttered television channels, these demonstrations were full of scripted imagery. Before those TV shows went on the air, the producers selected the women who screamed the loudest and gave them and others like them the most screen time, as if they were the ones who had won prizes. The demonstrations used a similar playbook.

Zelenskyy was concerned, too, about miners' demonstrations over unpaid back wages. The coal mining industry in Ukraine has traditionally drowned in debt. The president repeatedly demanded an answer about these debts from the regional leaders and the ministry. Once, he even went out by himself to speak with the miners demonstrating outside the presidential office, unexpectedly, without consulting anyone.

Zelenskyy insisted that the government provide any promised subsidies to the state mines, because the government owed the workers hundreds of millions of hryvnias for wages. And then, making an important distinction between state-subsidized mines and privately run mines, which were owned by some of the country's richest men, he said that these mine owners were obligated to pay their workers back wages, so that protesters would understand that the state had no role in private mining and they were being deceived by their private employers.

In that space where fiction meets reality, ideals meet cynicism, and permissiveness is confused with liberty, hundreds and thousands of people participated in endless protests, not only in Kyiv but also in cities and towns around the country, acting out their staunch opposition and natural resentments, but motivated basically by self-interest.

These supposedly ordinary people included the drivers of $200,000 John Deere tractors used to blockade the government district, asserting "the rights of poor farmers," and aggressive picketers "against increasing tariffs," sponsored by gas oligarch Dmytro Firtash, who profited directly from those low tariffs, siphoning cheap gas intended for the population to his businesses. There were also the marginalized radicals "defending" the Russian language from imaginary "nationalists"—a charge that had no foundation in fact but was often claimed by Russia.

Almost every demonstration was covered on social media or chats. By looking through multiple text messages and by checking out chat groups, it was possible to find out how much money people were being paid to participate in a demonstration, from $5 for a half hour to $35 for a whole day. So these so-called entrepreneurs could receive four times more in a month than their average monthly wage. (Sometimes the price of morality added up to slightly more than $1,000.)

Another reason for organized, and often massive, protests was the exorbitant taxes on new cars. The taxes on a new car in Ukraine were one and a half to two times more than, for example, in the EU. To get around the taxes, many foreign-registered used cars were brought into Ukraine, supposedly for temporary use by foreigners. But in fact, the vehicles were the unregistered property of Ukrainian citizens for personal use, resale, or disassembly for parts, imported without paying customs duties. The practice of owning used cars registered in foreign countries had been widespread since 2014; millions of vehicles had been imported under this scheme. I understood why many drivers in the poorest country in Europe were angry, but I also thought they were wrong to avoid taxes and import old, polluting clunkers. This was a matter that required a long-term institutional solution, and the government had already succeeded in addressing many of the issues. A generous penalty formula and regulations had reduced the number of unregistered cars from millions to hundreds of thousands.

In the same block, far from the Ukrainian parliament, another group of protesters, who called themselves "Ukrainian entrepreneurs," protested for months on end against proposed legislation that had already been delayed for a year without understanding its essence, warming themselves in the municipal toilets between demonstrations and abandoning their workplaces. No law would have harmed the small entrepreneurs as much as their voluntary absence from their places of business. The endless conflicts bankrolled by financial and political groups also worked to discredit the utility of genuine political protest as a powerful instrument of democracy.

———

My teacher Valentyna Datsiuk, from the Kherson Ukrainian-language high school, taught us a very important lesson that has stayed with me throughout my life. She told us that we needed to not only study literary, mathematical, and technical subjects, but also learn how to become the nation and country that, as Ukrainian citizens, we would all like to be. "Freedom has to be learned, too!" she said. That lesson captured my usually wandering attention during classes. Freedom is often associated with the absence of limits and rules, but there is a difference between freedom and permissiveness. Freedom presents the possibility of opening up and learning, of building a just and civilized society for everyone; therefore, freedom by definition always has boundaries and precise rules. Otherwise it turns into anarchy, where an absence of limits, disrespect for values, and nihilism are the rule. Democracy assumes that the freedom of one person ends where the rights of another begin. Democratic societies that are more evolved than Ukraine's understand this. When they forget this basic truth, they put themselves in peril.

Many of my classmates laughed at our teacher's remarks, but as a child raised in a family of Komsomol idealists, I did not. I reacted very differently. To illustrate her point, she told us the story about how our society's attitude toward sex had evolved after communism.

Everyone knew that "in the USSR there was no sex." Sex began to be openly discussed only after the creation of an independent Ukraine. A society that had been forbidden to speak, read, and think about sex suddenly was free to do whatever it wanted. A society astonishingly ignorant of basic sex culture went to extremes of sexual indulgence and suffered all its possible consequences: a surge of sexually transmitted diseases, an HIV epidemic, an increase in the number of abortions and teenage mothers due to rape, the proliferation of prostitution, and too-early sexual experience. What had previously been forbidden or socially unacceptable had become cool. However much I, a prim young girl, did not want to admit it, the examples my teacher cited were true.

Democracy with total permissiveness will implode, sooner rather than later. And yet, if a nation has long been forbidden from doing something and then, suddenly, what had been forbidden is allowed, it is natural at least for some people to let loose in the most self-destructive ways. We thought naively that once we achieved democracy it would just have its own momentum. We were wrong. Like other democracies with greater experience than ours, we learned that democracy has to be nurtured and cherished or else it will wither and die. A country like ours needs decades to learn the rules and habits of democracy, including mutual respect for our differences as well as accepting the bonds of our commonality as Ukrainians.

As we develop, the anecdotes and jokes demeaning women, Jews, Black people, and gay people will become incomprehensible and no longer funny. Then a woman will be beautiful thanks not to her youth and looks, but to her mind, energy, and wise smile. Then parliament will enact legislation to defend the victims of domestic violence, the police will not brush away like a bothersome fly the complaints of a woman beaten by her husband (what used to be thought of as a family matter), and those suffering from domestic violence will be unafraid to speak up. Then people will stop to pick up someone's carelessly dropped candy wrapper and won't spit out their chewing gum on the street. These are all rules and limitations throughout the civilized world because they preserve human values and allow people to live together as a community.

Similarly in a free society, we must learn that truth-telling binds us all together. It is a restriction, very strict and demanding, and also an opportunity to build democracy. We do not have the license to say anything or assume that anything goes. It is impossible to build a democracy without the freedom to speak the truth, but it is also necessary to have a commonly accepted understanding of what is true. Fake news erases the boundaries of truth, the boundaries of trust, and the boundaries of reality.

Fake reports in the media, fake demonstrations in the streets. Neither freedom nor democracy can be built around falsehoods. The only thing you can build with them is an illusory image of freedom, but over time society will either recognize that facade or collapse in on itself.

Zelenskyy believed that the new generation of Ukrainians, born after the collapse of the USSR, had a better understanding of independence and freedom. That this new generation was ready and able to build a strong state. He believed that declaring our independence from the Soviet Union and its outmoded ideology was the necessary foundation for a true Ukrainian democracy.

"Today an entire generation is already formed, born in independent Ukraine. For them, this is the normal way of things. For them there can be no other way. And this is marvelous. Because this generation is our intellectual pillar. The pillar of freedom, democracy, and development. They think differently, they think in a contemporary way, and that means Ukraine will only move forward," he said on August 24, 2019, the Independence Day of Ukraine, in the first year of his presidency.

CHAPTER 11

Disinformation Wars

We forget that information weapons have long been
more powerful in the world than nuclear arms,
because they are not banned.

—VOLODYMYR ZELENSKYY

(INTERVIEW, *AXIOS ON HBO*, JANUARY 23, 2021)

While disinformation, fake news, and propaganda have been around since the beginning of time, today, new technologies are helping it proliferate online, often drowning out responsible voices. Nowhere is this truer than in Ukraine.

Bot technology, which was developed in the earliest years of the internet, has more recently been put to nefarious uses. Unscrupulous actors are using social media algorithms to raise the popularity of particular kinds of inflammatory content and to spread propaganda.

For more than a decade, former Soviet bloc countries have played an important and disturbing role in developing bot and troll farms. Russian and pro-Russian Ukrainians, many working for the Russian Federal Security Service, have launched well-functioning bot factories, creating chaos, distractions, anger, and fear via numerous disinformation streams that now pose an integral challenge everywhere, in countries as different as Venezuela, Colombia, the United States, and the U.K.—not just in Ukraine.

This is how it works. We are spending more and more time online, reading posts, watching videos, and consuming more information than ever. We share them with our friends and tweet about them. Many people rely on social media for all their news. In this way we have created entirely new information ecosystems outside the traditional systems that include fact-checking procedures.

Bots pretend to be a person online. They take advantage of our already established social media networks and spread like wildfire on them, on Facebook, Twitter, Instagram, and instant messaging apps. The messages they push out are simple, precise, unambiguous, and convey a single thought. They are calibrated to produce the strongest emotions possible and elicit fear and confusion, creating havoc and causing considerable psychic damage to each of us, our loved ones, and people all over our country.

After Zelenskyy became president, it didn't take long for him to understand how dangerous these bot farms are and the peril they posed to Ukraine: "These are the challenges of today, and we must be prepared for them," Zelenskyy said in an interview with Interfax-Ukraine in February 2020. "In Ukraine, this is now a real business, a very serious business. Bot farms are a problem, whatever they are: for white or black, there is no difference. Because those who stand up for good, such as Ukraine's independence, in social media today may be against it tomorrow. Therefore, we must fight against such things. For the independence of the country, the independence of the individual, human rights must be fought in any way."

At that moment, Zelenskyy was speaking more broadly, meaning that not only Ukrainians but the whole world must learn to distinguish the line where freedom of speech ends and disinformation begins. To me, it seemed a very crucial point, because if we cannot decide on what is allowed on social media now, we will be unable to deal with even greater challenges in the future.

Bot farms were used to supplement and reinforce the methods used on the oligarch-owned television networks. They helped amplify the message of pro-Russian puppets brought to power by Moscow in different countries, influencing their politics and media. For Russia, the internet has been an important source of contemporary propaganda, and its use of the internet is analogous to the methods the Nazi propagandist Joseph Goebbels developed in the 1930s on the radio and in newspapers. As he once said, "If you tell a lie big enough and keep repeating it, people will eventually come to believe it." Nonsense remains nonsense in the singular. But when someone sends hundreds and thousands of nonsensical posts and commentaries to people's phones and computer screens, people begin to believe what they see.

Here is but one outrageous example in Ukrainian media: to undermine government land reform policies, an endless number of absurd stories appeared about Chinese people digging up and shipping out the famously fertile Ukrainian soil. The usual chauvinistic and racist Russian-style propaganda outlets promulgated and published these stories. Their purpose was to create doubt about these needed land reform measures—such as lifting the moratorium on the sale of Ukraine's agricultural land and investing in irrigation systems—which would help rid the agricultural sector of fraud and abuse and boost Ukraine's economy. In the same vein, other stories trumpeted that Zelenskyy was a pro-Russian president or controlled by oligarchs—anything that could undermine people's trust in him. By repeating such garbage over and over again, some were seeking political dividends. This fake news contributed to an oppressive political atmosphere and increased Ukrainians' disenchantment with their institutions.

I became deeply familiar with this type of "journalism" after I began working as President Zelenskyy's press secretary, not only watching what was done to the president and the First Lady, but also experiencing it myself.

Let me explain to you how these smear campaigns worked with one incident that I experienced firsthand. When the president and First Lady attended Japanese emperor Naruhito's enthronement ceremony in October 2019, they posted an official portrait to mark the occasion. The teams of people who operate bot farms immediately began to analyze how they could criticize the first couple, looking for anything to promote an impression that they were inexperienced and prone to mistakes.

There wasn't much that they could find in a photo, so they seized on the issue of the First Lady's formal gown, which was lemon yellow, and tried to turn it into a scandal. Hundreds of "experts" in Japanese protocol, who were really paid political bloggers (they earn from $150 to $500 or even more sometimes for their posts), shared photos with the comment that the First Lady of Ukraine violated protocol and offended the Japanese court and the people of Japan by wearing a lemon-colored dress. They pretended as if everyone knew this, but not the Ukrainian first couple. Their posts were supported by hundreds and even thousands of bots, which liked, shared, and commented. The social media posts rose in popularity (which is how social media works, Facebook specifically in this case). The topic went viral and spread all across the internet, making people believe that the first couple had made a gaffe and, worse, made Ukraine look bad. Then controlled online media outlets published short, sensationalized news pieces on this same topic, reaching a wide audience. At that point, supposedly independent media saw that the topic had gone viral and published pieces about how the first couple was being criticized. And that is how the topic became a huge story in Ukraine, dominating the information space for weeks, even though yellow is a perfectly fine dress color in Japan and no protocol had been violated.

In my own case, I was savagely attacked by means of bot farms for the two years I was press secretary. All sorts of absurd fake news circulated about me, so much so that another Iuliia Mendel whom I didn't recognize appeared in the cybersphere. It still haunts me now that my reputation has been so destroyed online by disinformation.

The attacks started almost immediately after I became press secretary. At the end of the first month, some bots claimed that I had used my first paycheck to buy a Mercedes with my last name emblazoned on the license plate. This lie went viral, and the President's Office had to refute it. But in between there were hundreds of these "news" items. Another notable example was from the last Normandy Format meeting in Paris in April 2021, where, due to an injured hand, I stuck my glasses into the front of my suit jacket. The etiquette experts erupted over this supposed breach online. The rest of the press office joked that no one cared about that Normandy meeting in Paris; the only story the country was discussing was the one about me and my glasses. There were hundreds of memes about it, and even the largest TV channel (owned by Kolomoyskyy) ran a piece on this. Absolutely exactly the formula that I told you: bots, so-called experts, fake media, sensationalized media, respected media . . .

From what I observed during those two years when I held the job of press secretary, there were bot farms run by a Ukrainian opposition party, unfairly mocking me for being stupid and unprofessional, and one by Russians, calling me ugly and trying to destroy my reputation.

The pro-Russian and Russian media also pushed the narrative that I was ugly and did not know how to behave or dress. Once, I posted a photo of me shaking hands with the presidents of Ukraine and Poland as part of a delegation. I was the only woman. My outfit was unassailable, so their criticism focused on my hair instead, attacking me for having a "nest" on my head, insinuating that my hairstyle was inappropriate.

Because I was a woman, my appearance became the news in the blogosphere and in online chat rooms, pushed by the infernal bots. (It is interesting to see that my successor as Zelenskyy's press secretary, a man, has been spared any of this silly attention.) It became clear that in carrying out these attacks, the Russians were taking aim at the presidency by attempting to discredit every member of Zelenskyy's team. Throughout it all I tried to stay calm, but it was difficult to endure the personal abuse.

There were many thousands of accounts and groups on social networks that were controlled by political consultants who shared pro-Russian positions. Most likely, these accounts were being managed from Russia. Pro-Ukrainian ideological groups were doing the same thing but clearly with a different political slant. Their tools created a different reality on the internet. They influenced even the most educated people with their pseudo-analytical thinking. They twisted the facts, creating disinformation. There were several purposes of these tools: first, to undermine any and all initiatives that could strengthen the state; second, to undermine politicians by attacking their popularity ratings; and third, to create a sense of hopelessness in people's minds, increasing their frustration and willingness to embrace whatever ideology was being peddled in beautiful, but empty, promises.

The power of Russian propaganda had been made evident to Ukrainians all the way back in 2014, during the Revolution of Dignity. Russia produced tons of unverifiable stories, accusing Ukrainians of violence and describing supposed internal conflicts inside the country. One of the most serious lies concerned an incident that took place in July 2014, when a passenger plane flying from Amsterdam to Kuala Lumpur was shot down by a Russian-made Buk missile while flying over eastern Ukraine. An international team of investigators later declared that the missile had been brought into Donbas from Russian territory and was launched by Russian-backed separatists. All 283 passengers and fifteen crew members on board the flight were killed. Nevertheless, the Russians produced stories accusing Ukraine of shooting the plane down, depicting the Ukrainians as the cruel killers and defending the mercenaries.

That same month, on July 12, 2014, right in the midst of a concerted Russian effort to tell the world that Ukraine was full of indiscriminate killers and terrorists, another fake anti-Ukrainian news story picked up steam. Russia-1 reported, "A refugee from Sloviansk recalls how the little son and wife of a militiaman were executed in front of her." The story alleged that Ukrainian soldiers had carried out a public crucifixion of a three-year-old boy in Sloviansk, a city of more than one hundred thousand people and one of the first towns attacked by Russia in the war in Donbas. The source for this preposterous tale was reported to be a woman, an alleged resident of Sloviansk, Halyna Pyshnyak.

"Women were gathered in the square because there are no more men. Women, girls, old people. It was a show trial. They took a three-year-old child, a small boy in shorts, in a T-shirt, and, like Jesus, nailed him to a bulletin board," a blonde was shown saying on camera. The level of detail, including what clothes the child was wearing, was what the audience found most convincing.

But in fact, no one had ever seen the event described. Opposition Russian journalists who had been allowed into Donbas at that time reported, but never managed to verify, the story. BBC journalists pointed out that there was no square by that name in the part of Sloviansk where the "crucifixion" allegedly took place. The blond woman herself appeared to be the wife of a person who had joined the Russian forces. Later, she moved to Russia, and in a subsequent video shown on opposition Russian TV, she complained that she was offended because local residents didn't like her.

Moscow seeded a similar story that took off in April 2021: Russian media widely reported that a Ukrainian unmanned aerial vehicle killed a five-year-old boy in Oleksandrivske village in the Russian-occupied territory of Donetsk region. Journalists investigating the incident confirmed that a child had indeed died in Oleksandrivske, but as the result of an explosion in the garage of a village resident. This additional context came only after the story was fed to the residents of the occupied territories and Russia as an example of the horrors and cruelty of the Ukrainian military, who were allegedly launching drones to kill small children. Even then, in April 2021, a year before the Russian invasion of Ukraine, the Russian propaganda machine was making absurd claims in order to generate hatred of Ukraine. In retrospect, it is clear that long before its recent invasion the Kremlin was already preparing its platforms for war.

In an interview with the online publication TheDigitalBrief .com, Edward Tufte, a professor emeritus of computer science, political science, and statistics at Yale University, cites a now famous quote: "There are only two industries that refer to their customers as 'users,' one is of course IT, the other is the illegal drug trade." A 2018 study by MIT researchers showed that fake news posts spread six times faster on Twitter than the truth. It certainly seems as if the same applies to other social media platforms as well.

The online system for spreading the Kremlin's narrative worked just as well, if not better, than it did on television. Almost every month, Ukrainian special services found online groups moderated from Russia. Then, in March 2021, the Security Service of Ukraine blocked the work of a bot farm with more than eighteen thousand accounts, which was managed by moderators from Russia and some pro-Russian political forces inside Ukraine. The bot farm organizers registered accounts using banned Russian email services. In October 2020, before the local council elections throughout Ukraine, the attackers began to spread their poisonous messages by developing fake opinion polls and artificially increasing the number of retweets and replies on individual opinion leaders' accounts and others that favored their point of view. Payments for the bot farms' services were made through banned Russian e-wallets, ensuring the anonymity of the clients paying to support these messages on social media. The cost varied depending on the complexity of technical tasks and the specifics of the target audience.

Later, in May 2021, cybersecurity specialists from the Security Service of Ukraine in Chernihiv, in northern Ukraine, shut down another bot farm, this one aimed at discrediting the Ukrainian authorities and inciting calls for internal revolt. The bots also claimed that some of Ukraine's transportation facilities had been mined, causing alarm and even panic. Russian bots also used messaging platforms to threaten people.

In March 2022, with the war in full swing in Ukraine, Hungarian communities living in Ukraine began receiving text messages with threats allegedly from Ukrainians. The bots were run by a resident of Kyiv whose group consisted of about twenty people with specified tasks and who had been hired by Russian contractors. The Ukrainian Security Service reported that the group was told to place information "inserts" aimed at inciting ethnic hatred in mass text messages containing threats to residents of one district of the Zakarpattya region, where many ethnic Hungarians live. Not surprisingly, this helped Hungary's authoritarian leadership justify its support of Russia in the 2022 war on Ukraine, and its pro-Putin prime minister, Viktor Orbán, won reelection by a large margin to an unprecedented fourth term in April 2022. Despite its membership in NATO, Hungary refused to consider sanctions on Russian energy, claiming it had to prioritize its own population, and banned the transportation of military weapons to Ukraine through its territory.

In retrospect, the Russian bots and trolls were working themselves into a frenzy in the months before that bloodcurdling morning of February 24, 2022, for one reason: they were preparing the Russian people—and the world—for their genocide in Ukraine. They had one blatantly false message that they pushed out endlessly: the Ukrainians were Nazis.

By inventing the myth of Nazi groups in Ukraine, Putin was trying to justify a military invasion of the country. For years, his propaganda fed people lies about Ukrainian Nazis raping, robbing, and murdering people in Donbas and about the threat they posed to Crimea. The propaganda spread stories about the drugs these supposed Nazis relied on in combat, about secret biolabs financed by the NATO countries and specifically by the United States to create dangerous viruses, and even about birds trained by Ukrainians to spread these viruses over Russia. Russian media made up countless absurd stories to prove to ordinary Russians who could not easily access information about Ukraine's democratically elected government that Nazis were in fact in control in that country. This was, of course, an implausible fiction. Ukraine had democratically elected a Russian-speaking president who had Jewish roots and Jewish family members who died at the hands of real Nazis. There was nothing even close to Nazism among the Ukrainian authorities. Yet Russian negotiators even absurdly demanded "denazification" of Ukraine during the peace talks, in perfect agreement with the bots and trolls. They, too, it seemed, had come to believe their own lies.

CHAPTER 12

The Fight of Our Lives

Life will win over death, and light will win over darkness.

—VOLODYMYR ZELENSKYY, SPEECH TO
THE EUROPEAN PARLIAMENT, MARCH 1, 2022

As I write this, Russia's horrific, genocidal war against Ukraine and its people still continues.

My mom called me on the first day of the invasion to say she was still going to the hospital where she works as a pediatrician. I wondered aloud whether it was a good idea for her to continue her ordinary schedule. "That's what I have to do," she said. "There are kids there. Who else should be with them?"

At the time, I thought that her hospital might have been a safe place to shelter. But I was wrong. Russians would go on to target hospitals and schools all over the country. The bombing of a maternity hospital in Mariupol on March 9, 2022, finally exposed the full criminal depravity of the Russian army to the world. Three people were killed and seventeen were wounded.

"What kind of country is this, the Russian Federation, which is afraid of hospitals and maternity hospitals and destroys them? Were there little Banderivtsi [right-wing Ukrainian nationalists]? Or were pregnant women going to fire at [the Russian city of] Rostov? Did someone in the maternity hospital abuse Russian speakers?" asked Zelenskyy in a scathing video, referring to the ridiculous Russian claim that they were conducting a special "denazification" operation in Ukraine. Zelenskyy had continued to broadcast a video every day to raise morale and keep the people of Ukraine informed of what was happening in the war.

For the time being, my mother's hospital remained intact. But along with the newborns and abandoned babies—yes, a gruesome phenomenon not often discussed—in her ward, she was hiding in a bomb shelter, enduring the invaders' attacks on her Russian-speaking city. Perversely, it's the Russian-speaking population, whom Putin has been trying to "save" for the past thirty years in all the republics of the former Soviet Union, who have been hardest hit in this war.

On another day, she wrote that there was a tank outside their window. "I don't know what to expect," my mother confessed. And a later note: "I'm on duty today. There is shooting in the distance." Every word cut my heart.

Kherson, my hometown in the south of the country, was the first and only large Ukrainian city to fall in those early days. Russian forces surrounded the city of around three hundred thousand people and wouldn't let anyone out or in. My relatives in the region were not only unable to leave their homes but often unable to reach each other, because the Russians had damaged cellular communications in the area. The Russians also tried to turn off the Ukrainian TV channels and turn on theirs. Russia knows so well that propaganda is a tool of subjugation.

After a week, it became clear that the city was on the verge of a humanitarian crisis. The mayor started handing out bags of food. Thirteen vans with humanitarian aid approached the city from the free Ukrainian side, but the Russians wouldn't let them in. People came out to protest.

The invaders came to the mayor to negotiate a policy: Russian humanitarian aid would come to the city only through the Russian-held Crimean peninsula, which borders on Kherson. The Russians delivered humanitarian aid several times, but almost no one took it.

The Kremlin even enlisted a young female politician from the area to help reassure the locals. She had helped the Russians during the illegal annexation of Crimea and then had a successful career in Russia. The Kremlin's political consultants were so insulated from reality that they apparently did not realize that for Ukrainians, this woman was a symbol of betrayal, not liberation. They did not understand that the "Russian world," so crudely and cynically imposed in the post-Soviet space, essentially had no hope of ever being accepted.

In response to the Kremlin's actions, Kherson protested. Angry, unarmed people confronted armed Russian soldiers. The Russians sometimes shot into the air to frighten people, then bombed civilian infrastructure—a school, a mall, residential houses. They brutally murdered several dozen citizens who had joined the Ukrainian territorial defense forces. And even so, the people of the city still took to the streets, wrapped in Ukrainian flags and singing the Ukrainian anthem. We were proud. I was proud. The whole world heard Kherson singing. A few days later, the Russians arrested four hundred protesters.

The Russians were taking over my hometown, my memories, and my future. I had been planning to bring home my fiancé, Pavlo, to meet my parents in the spring. At that moment I did not know if they were ever going to meet him, or if I would ever see them again.

But this personal tragedy did not compare to the horror being perpetrated in other Russian-speaking regions. Donbas, Kharkiv, and the Kyiv region were being attacked with devastating force. Soon we heard that the city of Mariupol in the southeast, with a preinvasion population of more than four hundred thousand, was in dire condition, surrounded by the Russian army and under siege. Many of the apartment buildings were bombed. All electricity and water had been shut off. There was a report that a six-year-old child had died of dehydration, and later on there were other reports of thousands dying. And we knew, with sickening certainty, that the number would go far higher.

All for what? Zelenskyy's words were lacerating: "Mariupol. A peaceful and hardworking city without any internal malice. It has been cordoned off. Blockaded. And purposely drained. Purposely tortured. Deliberately cut off from any communications. Deliberately blocked from access to food and water."

Mariupol's situation was a grim reminder of 1933, when Stalin's state-induced famine, the Holodomor, raged in Ukraine. But now, in 2022, there was not even any water. To save themselves, people melted snow and unscrewed the radiators in their homes, using heating water for drinking. The city had no electricity. There were days when the Russians bombed Mariupol every half hour.

At first the Ukrainian soldiers fought in the streets of the city, but then, facing an overwhelming assault by the enemy, they and numerous civilians, including children, took shelter in the vast Azovstal steel plant, where they were able to hold off the invaders for more than eighty days. Russian forces attacked and bombed them incessantly. Many defenders died or suffered grievous wounds that, due to lack of medicine, required primitive amputation without anesthesia. Yet they persevered, invincible. The whole world watched them, powerless and agonized at their fate until, finally, they were commanded to surrender in order to stay alive. The civilians who had remained with them were allowed safe passage out of the complex, but Russian authorities took the fighters and the wounded to the occupied territories as hostages. But to the world, they were heroes, holding off a huge Russian force, keeping them from fighting elsewhere, and giving the Ukrainians precious time to prepare for the battle of Donbas.

In the rest of the city, safe humanitarian corridors were also desperately needed. People, especially seniors, women, children, and the disabled, had to be evacuated. Food had to be brought in. People were dying not only because of the shelling. People were dying for lack of medicine and medical care for heart and asthma attacks and strokes—increased because of stress, especially among the elderly. People were dying in bomb shelters, now places of fear and death. Others died in their homes. Civilians and soldiers alike were being taken prisoner and murdered.

From the first days of the invasion, Russia was able to send missiles and bombs into cities all across Ukraine. The Russians reached the outskirts of Kyiv on the second day of the invasion. That was the moment when Pavlo and I left the city, just an hour before the Russians entered the northern district of Kyiv, and fled in our car to Lviv in the west.

The first battles began in Kyiv's Obolon residential area in the north of the city. The Russian advance was repulsed. But gradually the capital was nearly surrounded. The Russians savagely bombed many towns and villages in the region and inflicted terrible harm on their occupants. Bucha and Berdyansk were scenes of massacres and rapes; we lost contact with acquaintances from these places and still have no idea what has happened to them. Families fled, huddled together in their cars or on foot, hoping to escape the murder-lust of the Russians, later describing how they miraculously survived, sitting for hours in cellars or barns, or even covering themselves with a bathtub. But many others didn't make it.

The Russians brought death and terror with them wherever they went. The world watched, sympathized, provided humanitarian aid, and began sending some arms, but it refused to do more, although both President Zelenskyy and the entire Ukrainian diplomatic corps pleaded for greater military help. From the very beginning of the invasion, Ukraine begged for a so-called no-fly zone. This would mean that NATO planes would monitor any air movements over Ukraine, and if Ukrainian airspace was violated by Russian planes, NATO would have to react—that is, destroy the invaders. This would have helped stop the endless attacks from the sky on peaceful Ukrainians. But Western European and American political and military leaders feared that any direct combat between NATO forces and the Russians would trigger World War III.

Suddenly no one remembered that in 1994 we had given up our nuclear arsenal—the third largest in the world—in exchange for security guarantees from the United States, the U.K., and Russia, which included the promise to respect our territorial integrity. Each country had signed the Budapest Memorandum agreement, which our government thought would protect us. But when Russia invaded Crimea and Donbas, there was collective amnesia. Overnight, our territorial integrity was in shreds, and so were the security guarantees.

Threatening thug that he is, Putin warned that he would view such assistance as Western participation in war. To further intimidate the West, he put his country on nuclear alert and had his forces proactively bomb and then occupy Chornobyl and Zaporizhzhia, the two towns where Ukraine's largest nuclear plants are situated, terrorizing all of Europe. The staffs operating the reactors were taken hostage. For me, Putin resembled a reckless terrorist with a fully loaded grenade. And the West did its best not to irritate him.

Closing the skies over Ukraine was obviously something that would enrage Putin. But Zelenskyy continued to urge that course of action anyway, and with good reason: the Russians were pulverizing our cities and towns, reducing them to rubble. He asked NATO over and over again to do this, because he knew Putin's savagery was limitless and that Ukrainian men, women, and children would die. We had seen it before. Ukraine did nothing to provoke Putin's annexation of Crimea in 2014, his first invasion of our eastern region of Donbas in the same year, or his brazen large-scale invasion of all of Ukraine eight years later. The West kept trying to make sense of Putin logically, to predict his next steps, never seeing that his monstrous behavior had to be confronted and stopped. Murderous dictators, like terrorists and hostage takers, make decisions regardless of argument or logic.

Zelenskyy could not accept the West's reluctance to provide enough assistance to assure a military victory. He understood the need to use overwhelming force with Putin's army. In nearly every speech, he implored NATO to do more, and each time the Western allies demurred, afraid to provoke Putin. This Western logic struck me as curious. They were afraid to do more to protect Zelenskyy's homeland because they did not want their own countries to come under attack. The European nations are so close together, even interconnected. The war would affect everyone in Europe. If Putin took over Ukraine, there was no guarantee that he wouldn't immediately, or after a little while, go into neighboring Moldova, the Baltic states, Poland, or, for that matter, anywhere else. Putin had so little respect for the Western world order that it did not matter to him whether a country belonged to the EU or NATO. Poland knew it; the Baltic states knew it. His insane and seemingly insatiable imperialistic ambitions had no limits, and no treaties would protect any country at his doorstep. In fact, a victory in Ukraine would be an encouragement to go further.

Ukraine had been warning the West about this for years, but the West did not believe it. Political systems that get too comfortable often ignore dangers; history has shown this again and again. Now Zelenskyy was telling the world that this threat would endanger far more than just his own country. Ukraine was defending democracy and the values on which the entire civilized world stood, and it was fighting alone. In response, the West merely wrung its hands, preferring a defensive war against Russia rather than a decisive counteroffensive.

As the war intensified, Zelenskyy became angrier and angrier about the West's inaction. In his video address on March 4, 2022,

Zelenskyy called the NATO summit "weak" and "confused," and in response to the explanation that a no-fly zone would provoke Russian aggression, he said, "This is self-hypnosis. Of those who are weak, underconfident internally. . . . And what did you think about at that summit? All the people who will die starting from this day will also die because of you. Because of your weakness. Because of your disunity."

Zelenskyy's voice was always strong and became even stronger during the war. The war clearly divided reality into good and evil. There were no shades of gray. The war was here. "I do not know who you can protect and whether you can protect NATO countries. You will not be able to buy us off with liters of fuel for liters of our blood. Shed for our common Europe. For our common freedom. For our common future," Zelenskyy said.

Seeing that NATO could not be persuaded to close the skies, Ukraine then asked at least for warplanes, and we would "close the skies" ourselves. Once again, the United States thought that publicly providing NATO military aircraft to Ukraine would anger Russia. And there were other frustrations as well.

When in early March U.S. secretary of state Antony Blinken announced the green light to supply planes to Ukraine, Eastern Europe greeted the news with praise. But four days later, the tentative decision was reversed. The United States apparently thought it could not go beyond what its NATO partners were willing to accept. It could have supplied planes through a non-NATO country or even a private company. But that did not happen. Ukraine waited impatiently. We had to keep pressuring everyone, even at the risk of offending the Western countries that had really made an effort to remain united against Russia. Several days later, it was clear that no planes would be delivered in the near future. The skies over Ukraine remained open, and more Ukrainians died.

When I managed to unglue myself from the endless news feed about more Russian atrocities and murders, the media coverage surrounding us did not let us forget about the war for a second. Pavlo and I walked into one of the few open restaurants in Lviv—the western Ukrainian city was sheltering around two hundred thousand additional people displaced by the war—and tears suddenly came to my eyes. The room was subdued, peaceful, and there was a lovely smell of cooked food. There were people talking softly about the usual things, smiling, ordering coffee. The contrast was so marked after the endless sirens in Kyiv, after our forty-hour drive in an endless line of traffic across half the country, after the explosions that first woke us and made everything shrink inside. On our phone screens we watched lives being destroyed in other big cities, our people fleeing in terror and dying. And here tranquility still reigned, the restaurant using the same menu with the same design with long-standing Polish motifs, the same smiling waiters.

This juxtaposition of alternate realities is the constant experience of those who live through the horrors of war: the stark, continual contrast of death and life. We knew that our struggle was to preserve this normal life, and no one should be blamed for continuing a restaurant business, continuing to buy delicious food, continuing to smile and talk about inconsequential things. But in such surroundings, war, destruction, and death became even more present, bigger, and more horrific. I was choosing what to eat, and the tears blurred the menu's letters in my eyes. My friend went there with her family after they, too, escaped from Kyiv. Her sixteen-year-old daughter cried when she entered the restaurant. They had to leave immediately.

In an alleyway nearby, sheltered from the main roads, a men's formal clothing store remained open. Its interior was somewhat incongruously decorated with giant spools of thread. Two young girls were standing outside, talking about how they were such bad drivers that when they drove, they had to turn on their emergency blinkers. That was amusing teenage talk from another, more peaceful time. Inside my head, reality seemed to be fragmenting.

Far beyond this alleyway, in other parts of our country, right at the same time, tanks were running over people or crushing them in their cars. In Markhalivka, a village southwest of Kyiv, a fifty-four-year-old grandfather named Igor cuddled his cat, Marsik, after the Russians shelled his village and obliterated his home. All he had left now was the cat and two grandchildren. Neither his wife, nor his twelve-year-old daughter with disabilities, nor his mother-in-law, nor his two sons-in-law, nor his wife's friend had survived. There, beyond this alleyway, I tried to make out the faint cries from Mariupol, a city where people were dying from hunger, cold, and thirst. A local journalist from Mariupol wrote me, "We are desperate! We trust no one! We are begging for help!"

This is what every war looks like, everywhere and always. The line between life and death, the lack of information, the effort to survive while trying to maintain a normal life. It was impossible to see the war around us and to understand Russia's aggression and the West's reluctance. Meanwhile, everyone was sick with worry and trying to find a way to do something, anything, for the war effort.

Pavlo had wanted to enlist in the first days of the war, but he had been refused initially by the military registration office on the grounds that there were enough soldiers and volunteer veterans. So instead, he set to work on coordinating the humanitarian aid coming into Ukraine. Just when I thought he wouldn't go off to fight, he enlisted in a special forces unit and went into the thick of it. He felt it was the right thing to do. I was proud of him and afraid for him. I cried quietly and sometimes prayed. Pavlo is important to so many people, not just to me. I forced myself to think only of our military victory and our happy future together.

After the first night of combat, he wrote me: "It's a tough and dangerous experience, but on the front lines all senses are heightened and all unnecessary things fall away. The voice in my head went silent, and I was very focused, with all my senses sharpened. When the danger passed and my mind calmed down, I felt good. The guys congratulated me after the fight and accepted me as one of them." And then he sent me a picture of his left hand with a ring on his ring finger, just like the one he had given me, only a darker, masculine version. We weren't yet married, but that was Pavlo's way of showing me what I meant to him. It was the most emotional moment of my life.

As for me, I continued to do my reporting in a borrowed apartment in Lviv and the war continued. It has already brought monstrous destruction and taken tens of thousands of lives— men, women, and many, many children—and the toll may go much higher still. What the Russians have done to Mariupol, Sumy, Kharkiv, Berdyansk, Bucha, and a long list of other cities and towns has been seared in the world's conscience. Those names will continue to multiply, along with the rapes, tortures, murders, and forced deportations, not to mention the increasing numbers of refugees—unless the Russians are driven out.

Out of all this pain, though, there is one thing I do know: this war, like the fiery breath of an enraged dragon, has burned away all that was artificial and superficial in our lives. Through intense pain and sacrifice, it has brought back our understanding of our own value, made us see the good that we can create from unwavering unity and courage and from caring for one another. We have seen the immense power that we derive from learning to work together as a people and a nation.

We are facing the greatest test and are determined to show our strength. If some of us die in this struggle, others will be born with the same honor and the will to defend. We are always at the point of beginning. We Ukrainians will never give up— not to Russia, not to terror or any other evil. The spirit of freedom cannot be conquered by centuries of slavery, or by decades of abuse, or by murder, or by cynicism. I have always believed in Ukraine. And I always will.

ACKNOWLEDGMENTS

This book would not have been possible without long evenings of English lessons that my parents made me endure and for which they spent every last bit of their money—nor without their boundless dedication to my upbringing. I thank them first and foremost for teaching me to be strong and to be myself.

This book would not have been possible without President Volodymyr Zelenskyy, who for the first time created a transparent, competitive process for job applications in Ukraine, even at the highest levels, and chose me as his press secretary. He has been called Charlie Chaplin and Winston Churchill. But he is neither; he is Volodymyr Zelenskyy, just as his native Ukraine created him, a sincere leader of a modern European country.

A hearty thanks to my aunt, who has always given me so much care and love, and who is now living under Russian occupation, and to my husband, Pavlo Kukhta, whose support is invaluable in my life.

My sincere thanks to my agents, Amy and Peter Bernstein, for their indispensable guidance, and to an old friend and invisible angel, Ernest Schreiber, without whom this book would not have been possible. Thanks also to my editors, Julia Cheiffetz, publisher at One Signal, and Nicholas Ciani, for their thoughtful input and patience. My profound gratitude to Madeline and Steven Levine, who devoted sleepless nights to a thorough translation of my original version, and contributed many editorial suggestions in the shaping of the final manuscript.

And a special thanks to everyone who understands that Ukraine is not a country from the past. We are the future. We have broken the enchanted shackles of the post-Soviet space and have become a territory of freedom. And now the whole world knows—we are the realm of Light and Power.

ABOUT THE AUTHOR

Iuliia Mendel is a Ukrainian journalist who served as press secretary and spokesperson for Volodymyr Zelenskyy, president of Ukraine, from 2019 until 2021. Her extensive journalism experience on TV and in print media includes work for the *New York Times*, *Politico Europe*, the Atlantic Council, *Vice*, *World Affairs*, and *Der Spiegel*, among others. Since the Russian invasion of Ukraine, Mendel has contributed to the *Washington Post* and has appeared on CNN, MSNBC, Fox News, and other TV outlets, reporting from Ukraine. She lives in Kyiv, Ukraine, with her husband, Pavlo Kukhta, and their two cats, Marusia and Hooligan.